Answers

By

Ian Irons

Illustrated By

Rob Smith Jr.

I would like to thank my parents for having me and for being wonderful parents to my sisters and me.

I would like to thank my wife for picking me and then working together with me to build an incredible life. I love her very much.

I would like to thank my children for working so hard to become the people that my wife and I are proud of. We could not have imagined being the parents of finer people. We value, above all other things, the time we spent raising them.

Finally, I would like to thank my nineteen-year-old self for not killing me. Looking back, I am most grateful for that leap of faith. In the first God Moment of his life, that sad young man made the right choice.

FOREWORD

This book is a promise kept.

At nineteen, while at college, I formulated a plan to drink a bottle of Johnny Walker Red, slip into a warm bath, open my wrist with a pocketknife, and let whatever I was go back to whatever it had been. From this plan you might assume I was depressed—and you would be right. But I got into that mind-set in an unusual way. My life's hopes had not been recently dashed. My lover had not jilted me. I was not a morose person by nature—I loved to laugh and to make others laugh.

What made me want to destroy myself was the result of a calculation. The calculation was to determine if the pleasure was worth all the pain.

I had just recently begun to really push myself—test the limits of what I could do physically, emotionally, and intellectually—and was finding that in nearly every case I was coming up short. The expectations set in my genetics and my childhood were at such a high level that every time I took a measurement of my reality, the measuring tape read "failure."

I don't remember what caused me to do it, or the day or month I did it, but I do remember looking at a piece of engineering paper, the green kind with a grid of thin black lines, where I had listed my life's past, present, and expected future pleasures on the left side and pains on the right. Each item of pleasure and pain was accompanied by a weight from one to ten rating the importance of the item, and then a quantity of how many times I would experience that item. Each element was then scored with the importance multiplied by the quantity. I totaled the pain elements and the pleasure elements and saw that pain had more points—it was the clear winner on the ledger.

What the hell!

I had heard characters in movies, books, and plays exclaim that life wasn't worth living, but I had just proven it using standard accounting practices.

So, like the other times in my life when faced with bleak prospects and roadblocks, I began to look for a way around. And the Johnny Walker plan was the best I could come up with—until I randomly decided to have faith in myself.

I noticed most of the pain on my ledger came from my ignorance of myself, human nature, and how the universe worked, so I compiled that ignorance into a list of questions. Then, staring at that list of unanswerable questions, I wondered who possibly could provide profound and sincere answers. That someone had to have my absolute trust—it had to be someone I knew would give me the complete, unvarnished truth, as he or she saw it.

Because I trusted no one to be 100 percent honest, I could come up with only one answer: a fifty-year-old me.

I made a deal with myself. I would not end my life at nineteen if my fifty-year-old self would be able to answer the questions, disprove my accounting, and clearly show that life was not a negative-sum game.

Now I am fifty, and I have used my life as a laboratory to find the answers to these questions and lay them out in a way that I, at nineteen, would have understood. I have educated myself with an advanced degree, traveled, read, risked, tried, failed, tried and risked more and succeeded, raised a family, founded and grown a business, and survived melanoma. After thirty years I finally feel comfortable that the knowledge I have wrestled from the universe is what my nineteen-year-old self was after.

One ritual that kept me going was reciting a few lines from a Robert Frost poem in the blackness of my room, moments before I fell asleep.

But I have promises to keep,
And miles to go before I sleep,
And miles to go before I sleep.

My promise kept me alive, until I gained enough wisdom, strength, and honor to take its place. The promise was like the scaffolding around a building under construction. The building is complete enough, and with this book I keep my promise.

The answers I provide are of course my opinions—they represent a philosophy I developed called I-ism that recognizes at once the smallness of the individual and its priceless value.

I tried to fashion my answers into something that could be gulped down in less than three hours. I know that at nineteen, that was the limit of my attention span.

My greatest hope is that what I am handing to you is better than what was handed to me. May you go farther with it than I did—be better than me.

I wish you wisdom, strength, and honor, because it takes all three to move you forward. Your forward movement will give your soul the two things it needs: the pearls of true happiness that are yours to claim and the knowledge that you helped move our remarkable species forward.

CONTENTS

1 HOW DID IT ALL BEGIN?
I have a theory.

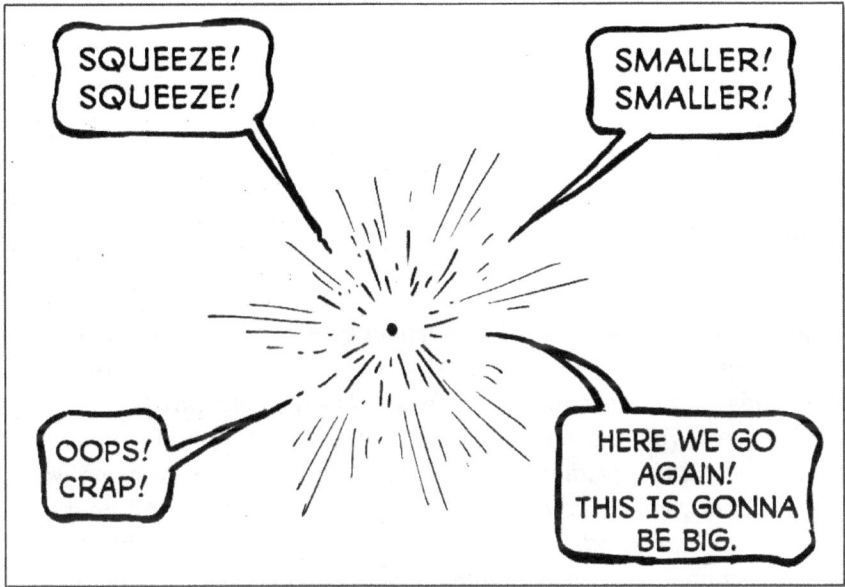

Life's but a walking shadow, a poor player,
That struts and frets his hour upon the stage,
And then is heard no more; it is a tale
Told by an idiot, full of sound and fury,
Signifying nothing.
—Shakespeare's *Macbeth*

This is truly a mind full, especially when "nothing" is just an ant's burp away from "everything."

Scientists currently believe that the universe started from nothing. I think that is basically true, in that a trillion-billion-gazillion dollars minus a trillion-billion-gazillion dollars is nothing. Something, which scientists are still trying to figure out, threw that nearly infinite "nothing" out of balance, and it became something; a small point of nearly limitless energy contained in a space smaller than an atom. Then, very quickly, in just a few Planck units (almost no time at all, really), some of the energy congealed into matter and antimatter, a battle between the two ensued, and the remaining winner, matter, spewed outward at incredible speed, creating both time and space. Observations show space to still be growing.

I might have gotten some of that wrong, but it doesn't really matter because it is just theory and it will surely be updated. The Norse people, the ancestors of some of the most sophisticated cultures in the world, had this creation theory:

Odin and Ymir

In the beginning of time, there was nothing: neither sand nor sea nor cool waves. Neither the heaven nor earth existed. Instead, long before the earth was made, Niflheim was made, and in it a spring gave rise to twelve rivers. To the south was Muspell, a region of heat and brightness guarded by Surt, a giant who carried a flaming sword. To the north was frigid Ginnungagap, where the rivers froze and all was ice. Where the sparks and warm winds of Muspell reached the south side of frigid Ginnungagap, the ice thawed and dripped, and from the drips thickened and formed the shape of a man. His name was Ymir, the first of the frost giants.

As the ice dripped more, it formed a cow, and from her teats flowed four rivers of milk that fed Ymir. The cow fed on the salt of the rime ice, and as she licked, a man's head began to emerge. By the end of the third day of her licking, the whole man had emerged, and his name was Buri. He had a son named Bor, who married Bestla, a daughter of one of the giants. Bor and Bestla had three sons, one of whom was Odin, the most powerful of the gods.

Ymir was a frost giant, but not a god, and eventually he turned to evil. After a struggle between the giant and the young gods, Bor's three sons killed Ymir. So much blood flowed from his wounds that all the frost giants were drowned but one, who survived only by building an ark for himself and his family. Bor's sons dragged Ymir's immense body to the center of Ginnungagap, and from him they made the earth. Ymir's blood became the sea, his bones became the rocks and crags, and his hair became the trees. Bor's sons took Ymir's skull and with it made the sky. In it they fixed sparks and molten slag from Muspell to make the stars, and other sparks they set to move in paths just below the sky. They threw Ymir's brains into the sky and made the clouds. The earth is a disk, and they set up Ymir's eyelashes to keep the giants at the edges of that disk.

On the seashore, Bor's sons found two logs and made people out of them. One son gave them breath and life, the second son gave them consciousness and movement, and the third gave them faces, speech, hearing, and sight. From this man and woman came all humans thereafter, just as all the gods were descended from the sons of Bor.

Odin and his brothers had set up the sky and stars, but otherwise they left the heavens unlit. Long afterward, one of the descendants of those first two people that the brothers created had two children. Those two children were so beautiful that their father named the son Moon and the daughter Sol. The gods were jealous already, and when they heard of the father's arrogance, they pulled the brother and sister up to the sky and set them to work. Sol drives the chariot that carries the sun across the skies, and she drives very fast across the skies of the northland because a giant wolf chases her each day. Moon likewise takes a course across the sky each night, but not so swiftly because he is not so harried.

The gods did leave one pathway from earth to heaven. That is the bridge that appears in the sky as a rainbow, and its perfect arc and brilliant colors are a sign of its origin with the gods. It nonetheless will not last forever, because it will break when the men of Muspell try to cross it into heaven.

The Norse story is prettier than the scientific story. There are hundreds of known creation stories. I've included one as a token for all the others. But I renounce all of them except the scientific story because, even though it is probably not correct, a new, more correct scientific story is always in the wings. I like that about science—it's brutally evolutionary.

It is a lot to wrap your head around: space and time not existing; space still expanding. At some point, gravity, electromagnetism, and the nuclear forces will once again gang up on the universe, it will all fall back home to that small point where space and time will evaporate, and the whole cycle will start again. That cycle is the heartbeat of God.

During each heartbeat, at certain places and times, life appears. The life we are familiar with is based on amino acids. We have some good theories on how amino acids can be created from a chemical soup when hit with the right amount of energy, and we have even more theories on how these basic components of life grow into higher forms, like amoebas, plankton, and politicians. But what is really missing is a line of reasoning that explains why all this stuff happens and what, if anything, we are supposed to be doing about it.

In the immortal words of Popeye, "I am what I am." I would add the word *barely*.

Let's first talk about the inevitability of life rather than the miracle of life. The odds against you being here are greater than winning the lottery every week of your life. Think about the odds against your ancestors one thousand generations ago meeting. Over twenty thousand years ago, a boy met a girl and they had a child, a baby girl, who grew up to be your ancestor 999 generations ago. Then, out of all the men in the world, she picked the one man carrying that one sperm that was destined to be your ancestor 998 generations ago. Now, each man packs about fifty million sperm into just one ejaculation. And each man, if he's lucky, will enjoy more than ten thousand ejaculations in a lifetime. So, the chances that a specific sperm will fertilize any female egg are fifty million sperm multiplied by ten thousand ejaculations, or five hundred billion to one.

A woman will ovulate about four hundred times. So, the chances that a couple will have a particular baby, out of all the babies that are possible for the couple to have, is five hundred billion multiplied by four hundred, or two hundred trillion to one. Going back just one thousand generations, the odds of all the correct sperm fertilizing the correct eggs in order to make all your ancestors (a requirement for your existence) is two hundred trillion

4

to the one thousandth power. The US Congress can't even imagine federal budgets that big. Now, take into account the odds against all your ancestors finding the one person needed to keep your lineage intact—for instance, the chances that your mother and father found each other, and their grandparents found each other, and so on, and so on, another 998 generations backward.

You really shouldn't be here. If you ever wondered why you are unlucky, realize that you depleted the vast majority of your luck just being born.

The most compelling reason that religious debaters use to combat the idea of abiogenesis (the study of how life on earth could have arisen from inanimate matter) is to say the odds against amino acids somehow combining to make a complex protein are just too high. May I remind you of the odds against the universe creating you?

Within the next ten generations, abiogenesis or something like it will allow us to create basic life. I also think that we will unlock the mysteries of force (gravity, electromagnetism, and the nuclear forces), and from this we will discover the building blocks and architecture of the universe enough to be able to travel freely through it. I am confident in this mainly because of the mind-boggling computing power that will become available to us in just a few more generations. We will be able to quickly simulate theories to see if they lead down blind canyons or reveal something worth investigating. Science and computing will allow us to worm our way to an incredible understanding of the universe devoid of the supernatural.

I hope we are smart enough to keep the computers away from the weapons, because if we are, in ten generations our kindergarteners will all be taught the same evolving creation theory, sans the obligatory imaginary friend for grown-ups.

So, in summary, of course I do not know how it all began. Anyone who claims to know is selling something.

2 DOES GOD EXIST?

Yes, but probably not the God you are thinking about.

Like many people, my first exposure to God was from church; in my case, Methodist. Being a Methodist is like being a churchgoing agnostic. The gospel is taught as sort of guideline. From this church and from the Bible, I gleaned an image of God as an all-powerful, all-knowing, tough-loving, imaginary friend that decided whether you were to be rewarded or punished for eternity based on how you lived your life. Even at the age of twelve, I understood that this idea was a powerful tool for keeping people in line, but it always rang hollow for me. I simply could not "buy in" to the whole concept of the soul, heaven, hell, and the supreme justice of God, because nothing in my short life up to then provided much evidence. In fact, I had already seen loved ones die, injustice, cruelty, and the randomness with which nature dealt out death.

So, over many years, especially in my thirties, I began reading about the world's religions and took an interest in anthropology. I found that nearly every culture created God in its own image to provide whatever cement was necessary to bind the culture together. The God of each was different, custom made to suit the culture, climate, geography, and time. The God most people are familiar with was created by humanity, not the other way around.

God was created at the exact moment a human first consciously solved a problem. Two things must happen to solve a problem: the problem must form in the mind and be accompanied by an emotional, gut need to smite it with a solution. The gut's need to keep the mind's perspective of the universe in simple, gapless, pristine order is the primary need for God, and is the wellspring of science.

Many thousands of years ago, humans coexisted with the world on a purely instinctual level like any other living thing. But through a series of evolutionary pratfalls, the brain was "gifted" with the basic ability to reason. This ability to reason was called into play by the instinctual animal, just like an adrenaline gland is summoned in the face of stress. From evolution's perspective, the species had taken a major step in moving forward and up. But something else important had happened: a hole in human consciousness had been opened which would never be closed. The insatiable need to fill that hole would drive the human species forward at such an evolutionary pace that humans would soon control every other species in the world and look further. So in that sense, the hole was a productive thing. But that hole in the soul is not only the major wind in our evolutionary sail, but the major source of individual and cultural pain and shame.

Eons ago, humans were trudging around, living their short, hard lives, eating, sleeping, crying, farting, bearing young, happy in their thoughts equivalent to those of a modern-day hamster. But one day, some young innovator, eager to take revenge on a rival, picked up a rock or a stick or a bone and realized that it could be used to dash out the brains of said rival. A problem (the rival's existence) and its solution (the end of the rival's existence via state-of-the-art weaponry) came to live in a human brain. As soon as the ability to question and logically answer popped into existence, the condition of having a question without an answer existed. At that moment, the need for God sprang into existence.

Humans have always been, like all other known animals, basically instinctual. Our habits govern our daily and hourly lives. We engage our ability to reason only when our nature calls for it. The most highly evolved of us may reason through 10 percent of our day. The rest of us respond to the alarm clock, traffic, conversation, lunch, and so on, with 98 percent instinct and 2 percent reason (about twenty-nine minutes of hard thinking per day). I am not counting the reasoning time spent on a problem at hand, like solving a puzzle or doing your job or trying to figure out how to get through the next traffic light. I am referring to the time spent thinking about **why** you should do the puzzle, or **if** you should change jobs, or **why** you are in such a hurry in traffic. But even though we govern ourselves only a fraction of the time with reason, this amount of time is enough to pry open our nature and plant questions. If the questions are not addressed somehow, unhappiness ensues.

Although animals like apes, dolphins, and squirrels are far more instinctual than humans, they can reason. I have seen a squirrel sit quietly and ponder. It may have been thinking about how nice the breeze was, or how a rock was a lovely shade of yellowish brown, or it may have been thinking of a way to make its balls stop itching. If that squirrel can have thoughts like these, then there is definitely a squirrel god (a god by my definition, anyway, which we will get to later) that each squirrel thinks about in its own way. Each squirrel has its religion, a way of feeling and thinking about itself and its surroundings. Even if they don't build little squirrel churches or go to war with one another over subtle differences in their theologies, it's still possible that squirrels possess the framework of thought that can be called religion.

What I am saying is that the need for religion and God is basic to any life form with the ability to ponder, and the need for religion is basic to the human condition. History proves this. Religions have been created in nearly every known culture. They have been created in every language, on every continent, and in every time period since humans have had the ability to reason. The same can be said of clothes and weapons. So, if we can reason that clothes and weapons have come in very handy, and can even be said to be requirements of civilization, then it is not a stretch to say that religion has been a requirement. In other words, throughout time it has been as important to answer questions as it has been to protect our bodies from the elements or bonk someone on the head with something more compelling than our fists.

At some point in our history, the comfort brought by believing the world worked a certain way, not because we had proof, but because it pleased us to believe that way, became very important to the bulk of humanity. This comfort was based on simply believing a certain way, and the popular support of the beliefs was not based on scientific reasoning, but rather on how many other people shared and supported the beliefs. The sharing of these beliefs wove people together. If one group of people discovered another group that did not share the same beliefs, they were either shunned, converted, or annihilated—God save their souls (I will define *soul* later).

God provides comfort because it (yes, God is an "it") answers questions that gnaw at your soul. Even if the answers are silly, if they are rich enough in detail or prose or imagery or humor, they satisfy. Reasonableness is not required.

If a religion successfully offers comfort to enough people, it can provide a guiding structure to the community, so where there was no moral north and south before, there suddenly is. Not only are north and south defined, moral compasses can be issued and each person's way judged. You have yourself a culture.

A really good religion must be filling and healthy. It must fill the void in the human soul, and it must provide a healthy moral

9

structure on which a sustainable culture can be created and evolve. Providing comfort to the individuals of a culture is a key requirement. And providing a strong foundation for long-term, sustainable cultural evolution is the other requirement. All religions to date have done a mediocre job.

The God I learned about did not answer my questions. In fact, I felt that the God I learned about was patronizing and completely unfulfilling. I went in search of a God that I could *really* believe in.

So I read and thought and read and thought and read. Years and years passed.

I ran across great quotes, like this one from Don Cupitt's *After God*: "*Just as the best way to conquer Satan is to give up the belief in Satan, so the quick way to save the world is to give up believing all the ugly old doctrines that made us feel that we are miserable sinners, and that life as a whole is unsatisfactory.*"

And this quote from Boethius, a Roman born around 480 AD: "*As far as you are able, join faith to reason.*"

One day, on a walk, I finally found God. I was looking at the early full moon in the waning daylight and realized that the moon and I were both doing our jobs—it was creating the tides and a million other things and I was digesting my dinner and producing methane. And we were both important. We were both doing God's work. We were both part of God. God was all around me all the time.

So, back to the question: does God exist? Yes. God exists.

God exists because God is not a character in an old book; God is not a metaphor. God is not the God of the Jews, or the Christians, or the Muslims—that God is a metaphor.

God is the nothing we started with, the everything that is here now, and the nothing that it is trying to become again. God is nothing more than a nice, short word for everything, everywhere, for all time, even before there was time. God is the real, tangible, physical everything. God is the "it".

This definition of God has one very important quality: God includes you—from the cells in your body to the thoughts in your head. You are a part of God.

Believing in this real God is like believing in algebra. It is not a question of believing, but simply ever-varying levels of understanding (or misunderstanding, I should say). The more you understand about yourself, why you do certain things, the more you will understand God. And you will never understand God fully. You and I are too puny. An ant will never understand Scrabble, and we, on our current evolutionary rung, will never understand God. But we can understand parts of parts, and we can put those together for a glimpse.

If you think about God in this way, a new world opens up. The major religions become meaningful, important, and sublime because of the rich metaphors they use to help explain God and the tools they provide to foster an ever-growing relationship with God. Praying feels better because you are talking to something *real*, not a character in a passion play. Prayer becomes self-hypnosis, optimism therapy, and a slightly one-sided dialogue with the universe. Prayer becomes a powerful source of strength that you can draw on at any time.

So, when asked if I believe in God, I answer, "Of course I believe in God—I just don't understand it." Which brings me to the answer of the next question.

3   WHAT IS THE PURPOSE OF LIFE?

A life's purpose is to create a subsequent generation that is more adapted to survive and thrive than the current generation.

God is seeking balance so that it can again be zero, perfect and blissful, infinite in scope, but null. God aches for eternal peace.

Now, if you were God and had been trying to achieve perfect balance time after time after time, only to collapse back into yourself in a less-than-perfect arrangement and inevitably bang out again, wouldn't you try to shuffle yourself more and more randomly on each bang, until finally you came together in a perfect arrangement? I know that is exactly what I would do.

What is a good randomizer? Proponents of quantum mechanics believe that the universe is random. But because quantum mechanics is a scientific field that did not exist three generations ago, I think it is safe to say that their judgment that quantum mechanics is unpredictable really just means that it seems random to them, kind of like how keeping a houseplant alive seems random to me. I can't think of a better way to stir God in a completely random way other than to create life that is self-aware and selfish and let it do its worst.

The second law of thermodynamics can be stated as "the entropy of an isolated system always increases or remains constant." *Entropy* is the classy word for the tendency of things to fall apart. Ice melting in a glass, neatly combed hair getting mussed by the wind, and an old lady's hip joint are examples of things attacked by entropy. When you toss a bolt with a nut screwed onto it up in the air a few million times, the nut will unscrew itself from the bolt. If you toss a nut and a bolt up into the air a few million times, the nut will never screw itself onto the bolt.

Nothing is immune from entropy. It is a universal force and God's main weapon in achieving a final, peaceful rest. But so far it has not been enough. That's why life is so important. Life is an anti-entropic force. Beavers assemble dams. Bees build hives. Congress writes bills. Plants create complex biological structures from nothing more than dirt, water, and sunshine. People build cities. Life is the single greatest random force against entropy. Life's struggle against entropy enhances the universe's random trajectory.

Life's force is not diametrically opposed to God's entropic force. Life does not undo God's entropic force. God attempts to mess up the universe, and life applies its own random order, which is really just another force messing things up. Life's force may be counter to God's entropic force, but it is still an entropic force of its own.

From God's point of view, life is an entropy enhancer—a randomizing condiment.

Life exists because God is trying to rearrange itself into a perfectly random arrangement so that it can one day collapse in on itself in perfect balance to achieve perfect, blissful nothingness. The purpose of life is the keystone in achieving perfect randomness.

Human life is about placing the next generation into a better position to more effectively battle entropy. If we could talk to animals and plants, I think they would claim the same purpose. The purpose of your life is to do your part in this great battle. As you will see later, we have some wonderful things in our future if we continue this great battle.

The time you spend actively searching for your place, with a passionate yet open heart, will be the most transformative time of your life. It is during this time that you must allow the universe, and people's ideas in particular, to gain entry to your core, your very soul, for your evaluation. Spit out the ideas that lack merit, especially if they are popular, and embrace and refashion the ideas that truly intrigue you. Your purpose is just lying there, waiting to be found, like an old person who has fallen and can't get up.

Finding where you fit in this great battle is the purpose of your life. Your part may be an idea you have, or something you create. Or it may be that your part is to invigorate and inspire another to create. Only you will know; and you will know you have found it in much the same way you know you are in love—you will just know.

4 ARE MY RELATIONSHIPS WITH PEOPLE IMPORTANT?
Yes, very.

People are just another part of God. You are just another part of God. But because you can exercise great power over yourself, you are the most consequential part of God you will ever deal with. If you can maximize your wisdom, strength, and honor, you will exert great force over your animal self, and, consequently, the people around you will be drawn to your strength and the direction you are going. To change the world, you start by changing yourself, and then leading the people around you to a place that they could not get to on their own.

The first reason that other people are important is you need their knowledge. You cannot learn in a vacuum. Most of the knowledge you have, and will ever have, came from someone else discovering it, or at least learning it and passing it on to you. Without knowledge, you cannot gain wisdom, and without wisdom, your life will be dreadfully lacking in meaning and quality.

The second reason other people are important is that any large work must be done by a large group of people. Brainstorms occur in individuals, but "work storms" are only possible with large groups of people.

A Brief History of the Individual and the State

The wilder tribes among the Native Americans considered it weak-kneed and unseemly to preserve food for the next day. Food preservation displayed a lack of confidence in your ability to get food tomorrow; in other words, only pussies planned ahead. One day, an individual convinced enough people in his clan that storing food was not just for pussies, but would enable them to out-survive a competing clan. Knowledge of the hunger to come in the future and a willingness to plan ahead enabled these early people to prevent the hunger. The cost was high—metaphorically, they were expelled from the Garden of Eden.

It is believed that while men hunted, women discovered agriculture; more probably, an individual woman discovered how seeds she had scavenged grew new plants when carelessly discarded in good soil. The cultures that learned to value agriculture more highly than hunting were the first to create civilization—speech, agriculture, and writing. It took a string of strong individuals many generations to convince the clan to value these new foundations of civilization over just hunting, gathering, and surviving.

Man, said Ben Franklin, is a tool-using animal, and since human skills and natural resources are diversely and unequally distributed, a people may be enabled, by the development of specific talents or by proximity to needed materials, to produce certain articles more cheaply than their neighbors. It took only one extraordinary individual in each clan to have an epiphany regarding how the clan could better make use of the world. If, in sharing the insight with the clan, the person believed he would be enriched, the insight was shared and the whole clan was enriched. If the person believed he and his idea would be abused, he kept his mouth shut. Villages that rewarded individual epiphanies advanced a little faster than the others.

Specializing tribes or villages sometimes acquired the names of their industry (Smith, Fisher, Potter, Hooper, etc.), and these names in time were attached to specializing families. A system of barter or trade grew, and money was developed. Cattle were used as money before coins because they had a standard value, they bore interest through breeding, and they were easy to carry, since they transported themselves. The word *capital* goes back to the Latin *capitale*, and this in turn derives from *caput*, meaning head— i.e., of cattle.

Extended families, or clans, banded together into tribes through the connections of their individual leaders. Tribes found safety and power together as states through the connections of the individual leaders of the tribes.

States and nations now compete for dominance of the earth, and today we have reached our pinnacle of civilization with the creation of the United Nations, where the world's leaders, individuals representing every major power on the planet, can come together on a regular basis and lie to each other.

In every major phase of cultural evolution, an individual made the first step, and probably was also then denigrated, maligned, insulted, and finally had the fruits of the step stripped away. Cultures that encouraged individual exceptionalism thrived, while cultures corrupted by centralized power and the inevitable thwarting of individual exceptionalism withered and morphed into cultures that again promoted individual exceptionalism.

As William Durant put it in *The Story of Civilization: Our Oriental Heritage*:

> *Darwin thought that the perfect equality among the Fuegians was fatal to any hope of their becoming civilized; or, as the Fuegians (indigenous inhabitants of Tierra del Fuego) might have put it, civilization would have been fatal to their equality.*
>
> *Communism brought a certain security to all who survived the diseases and accidents due to the poverty and ignorance of primitive society; but it did not lift them out of that poverty. Individualism brought wealth, but it brought, also, insecurity and slavery; it stimulated the latent powers of superior men, but it intensified the competition of life, and made men feel bitterly a poverty which, when all shared it alike, had seemed to oppress none.*
>
> *Perhaps one reason why communism tends to appear chiefly at the beginning of civilizations is that it flourishes most readily in times of dearth, when the common danger of starvation fuses the individuals into the group. When abundance comes, and the danger subsides, social cohesion is lessened, and individualism increases; communism ends where luxury begins. As the life of a society becomes more complex, and the division of labor differentiates men into diverse occupations and trades, it becomes more and more unlikely that all these services will be equally valuable to the group; inevitably those whose greater ability enables them to perform the more*

vital functions will take more than their equal share of the rising wealth of the group. Every growing civilization is a scene of multiplying inequalities; the natural differences of human endowment unite with differences of opportunity to produce artificial differences of wealth and power; and where no laws or despots suppress these artificial inequalities they reach at last a bursting point where the poor have nothing to lose by violence, and the chaos of revolution levels men again into a community of destitution.

Hence the dream of communism lurks in every modern society as a racial memory of a simpler and more equal life; and where inequality of insecurity rises beyond sufferance, men welcome a return to a condition, which they idealize by recalling its equality and forgetting it poverty. Periodically the land gets itself redistributed, legally or not, whether by the Gracchi in Rome, the Jacobins in France, or the Communists in Russia; periodically wealth is redistributed, whether by the violent confiscation of property, or by confiscatory taxation of incomes and bequests. Then the race for wealth, goods and power begins again, and the pyramid of ability takes form once more; under whatever laws may be enacted the able man manages somehow to get the richer soil, the better place, the lion's share; soon he is strong enough to dominate the state and rewrite or interpret the laws; and in time the inequality is as great as before. In this aspect all economic history is the slow heartbeat of the social organism, a vast systole and diastole of naturally concentrating wealth and naturally explosive revolution.

Your relationship with other people, the "individual–state" relationship, is what makes the human world go around. Since humanity has the power to destroy itself and most life on earth, that relationship is more important than how well you play music, or understand math, or write software. If you underestimate the power or consequence of this relationship, you are dooming yourself to a second-rate life. And because it is a bona fide miracle that you are here at all (see answer to "How Did It All Begin?"), you use yourself poorly if you undervalue this relationship.

A good relationship with people is a lot easier if you have a good relationship with yourself. The quality of your self-relationship is in direct proportion to your store of strength, honor, and wisdom.

Your strength is measured by how much punishment you can take and still remain responsible and loving to yourself and others. Your honor is measured by how well your actions match your words. Your wisdom is measured by the accuracy of your perception of reality through time, especially where it pertains to you.

Do not underestimate the power of prayer in achieving more strength, honor, and wisdom. When you pray to the tangible God, a very useful thing happens—self-hypnosis, because you are saying out loud what you want and what you need from God to get it. Repeating a prayer several times a day for weeks will cause those thoughts to become part of you—the part of you that the priests of psychology call the subconscious. So whatever you are after, whatever your goal is, it will not just remain a want—it will become a need, and you will naturally reprioritize your resources to get it. This is a simple way to make yourself stronger, and all it takes is a commitment to pray. If you want to earn a spot on a team, or pass a class, or make a sale, and if you isolate what you need from God to achieve your goal and pray, your chances of success will skyrocket. You will naturally rearrange your priorities to achieve the prayer's object. You will prepare yourself hour by hour and day by day to seize any opportunity that will take you closer to your goal. Prayer prepares you to be ready to seize opportunity. Luck favors the prepared.

If you have more general wants—for instance, comfort, or security, or forgiveness—Jesus Christ provided a very nice prayer during his Sermon on the Mount. This is the version I learned in Sunday school.

Our Father, who art in heaven,
Hallowed be thy name.
Thy kingdom come,
Thy will be done,
On earth as it is in heaven.
Give us this day our daily bread,
And forgive us our trespasses,
As we forgive those who trespass against us.
And lead us not into temptation,
But deliver us from evil.
For thine is the kingdom, and the power, and the glory
Forever and ever.
Amen.

I remember at the age of ten not knowing what *hallowed* meant, so I thought everyone was saying Harold. For two years I thought God's name was Harold. It did not help to hear kids swear "Jesus H. Christ!" This just reinforced my mistake because I thought that the H stood for Harold. Religion can be tricky.

Although I still find this prayer powerful and I say it from time to time, I prefer my personal prayer to God.

God,
You are my creator
And planned me from the start.
You gave me curiosity
To find your hidden heart.
With wisdom, strength, and honor
I'll love both friend and foe,
And hone my soul till my last breath,
When back to you I'll go.

The most fruitful and rewarding relationship you will ever have with God will be through your relationships with people: your family, your friends, strangers, and even enemies. Every one of these relationships is limited in its quality and strength by the quality of who you are and how much strength, wisdom, and honor you have. Build these qualities within yourself. Use them to create strong relationships with people and you will be a happy and fulfilled child of God.

5   WHY DO I SENSE THAT THERE IS MORE?
Because there is—and knowledge of it would be too hard to bear.

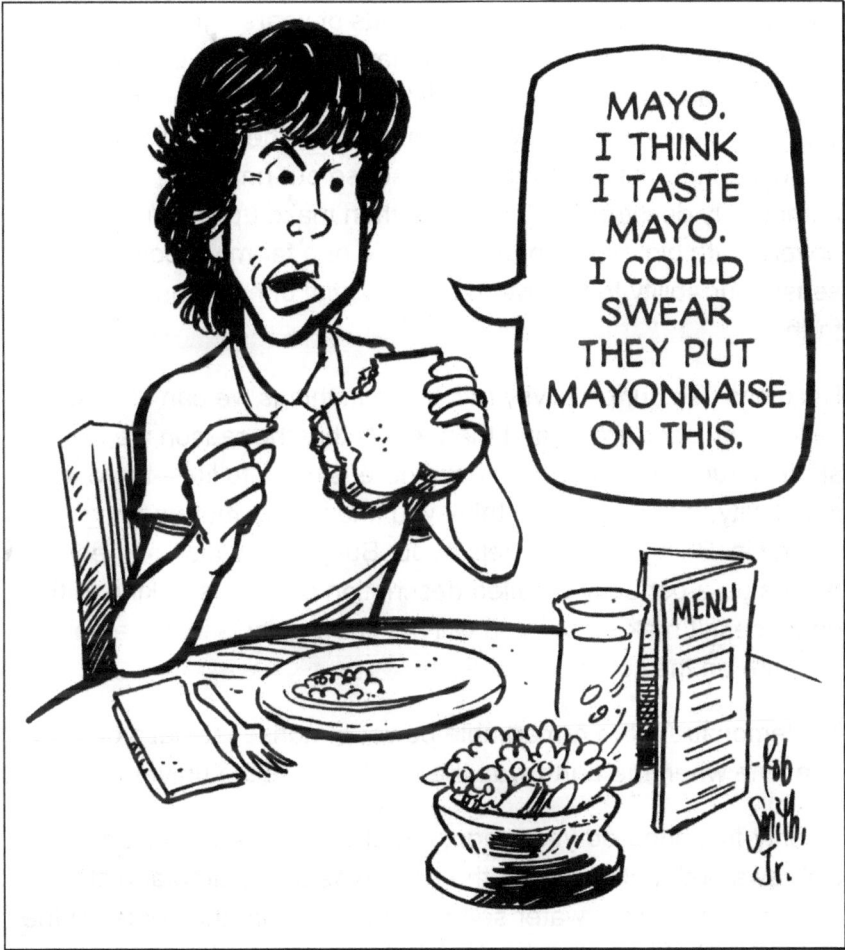

Daniel Defoe's Robinson Crusoe reflected, "*How infinitely good the Providence is which has provided, in its government of mankind, such narrow bounds to his sight and knowledge of things; and though he walks in the midst of so many thousand dangers, the sight of which, if discovered to him, would distract his mind and sink his spirits, he is kept serene and calm by having the events of things hid from his eyes, and knowing nothing of the dangers which surround him.*"

Religions through the ages have capitalized on the uniquely human sense that there is more to reality than what we can see, hear, touch, smell, and taste. This was practically demonstrated to us when we first discovered thousands of years ago that other animals have more acute senses than we do. Dogs can out-smell us, birds can out-see us, and most animals can out-hear, out-touch, and out-taste us. When compared to the rest of the animal kingdom, in terms of being able to sense our universe, we are pathetically destitute. But we more than make up for our sensory poverty with big, heavy brains capable of a far more powerful sense: our ability to believe in the potential of nonsense to be truth.

Religions use our proclivity to believe in things we can't sense to sell us *any* good story, and then tell us that the reason we feel the story is true is because we know there is more to life—there is spirituality. It feels good to think you know what that nagging feeling is. Being spiritual feels good. But just because someone makes up a perfectly detailed description of what is lurking in the dark doesn't make it so. You will not know what is in there until you turn on the lights.

To demonstrate the remarkable power of nonsense, let's go back to a time when the earth was the flat center of the universe.

Twenty-five hundred years ago, the ancient Mesopotamians and Hebrews both believed that the earth was a flat, circular disk surrounded by a saltwater sea and that we were the center of the universe. That is something I might have dreamed up when I was ten.

Twenty-three hundred years ago, Aristotle provided observational evidence that the world was not flat but rather a sphere. One piece of evidence was that the border of the shadow of earth on the moon during the partial phase of a lunar eclipse was always circular, no matter how high the moon was over the horizon. Only a sphere casts a circular shadow in every direction, whereas a circular disk casts an elliptical shadow in all directions, apart from directly above and directly below. I can tell I lost some of you there. Twenty-three hundred years ago, almost *everyone* was lost.

Nineteen hundred years ago Ptolemy advanced many arguments for the sphericity of the earth. Among them was the observation that when sailing toward mountains, they seem to rise from the sea, indicating that they are hidden by the curved surface of the sea. Ptolemy derived his maps from a curved globe and developed the system of latitude and longitude.

Just over six hundred years ago, many crews of sailors repeatedly sailed around the world without falling off, and the theory of earth's un-flatness began to garner popular support.

Five hundred years ago, Copernicus theorized that the center of the earth was not the center of the universe.

Fewer than four hundred years ago, Galileo, a believer of Copernicus who had a weak telescope (less than thirty power) and a strong brain, not only proved that the earth was not the center of the universe but fathered modern science by marrying disciplined theory and structured experimentation.

Throughout this evolution of thought, our ability to embrace a view of the universe that conflicted with what our instinct was gathering from our senses served as a constant beacon. Our ability to take an anti-sense or a nonsense perspective and test it against a non-instinctual standard allowed us to earn an understanding of the universe that could not be directly sensed—it could only be understood. Understanding became our greatest sense. It had been shown that by demoting our primary senses to secondary status and promoting our mind's ability to see to primary status, we could attain a greater understanding of the universe.

We had to invest time and energy in nonsense to see which nonsense was a dead end and which led to cosmic illumination.

Nonsense is like gold ore. You might have to dig one thousand tons of dirt to get one ounce of gold. You must believe in the task enough to invest the work, and you have to be disciplined enough to discard the nonsense that, after testing, yields no value. But after the hard and disciplined work, you have gold. Knowledge is mined the same way.

It is important to note that during the voyage from the flat center of the universe to the round, mildly important planet, religious culture fought the progression the whole way. Nonsense had been its birthright, its realm, and it was unwilling to suffer competition. Religion had in all cases amassed power though trading in nonsense and would do anything to maintain that monopoly. More important to it in maintaining the monopoly of nonsense was its opposition to subjecting nonsense to reasonable testing and then discarding the nonsense that was found wanting. If everyone adopted this kind of radical thinking, the franchise of religion would be kaput.

Until the 1960s, when photographs became available, the earth could not be seen to be round and could not be seen to be just another planet. We had developed mathematical and physical models and taught these models to generations of our youth, so that the idea of a round earth and an earth that was just another planet became commonly understood. So when the first photographs of earth were published, they were not awesome because they were shocking; they were awesome because they were beautiful.

Humanity's superpower is our ability to rise beyond our senses and take nonsense seriously. It is also our biggest weakness. Our natural gift to believe in nonsense is married to our natural sloth, which retards the questioning of that same nonsense. It is not our nature to question and analyze nonsense. This is a skill that is cultured and grown with discipline. Luckily, our urge to discover the innermost workings of the universe is just slightly stronger than our urge to invent and then hold tightly to dogma.

Our proclivity for nonsense enables us to believe in and even find great joy in literature, art, Santa Claus, God, the devil, luck, ghosts, the Loch Ness monster, honest politicians, Bigfoot, and the afterlife. But our ability to believe in nonsense is also a major weakness, because it is the best way one person can manipulate another.

A great example of this is our ability to believe that each of us can beat the natural law of statistics. I have purchased lottery tickets, the kind where the odds are fifteen million to one against winning. But even at those odds (and "one in fifteen million" is very nearly the same as "no chance in hell"), I still felt I had a real chance. I felt that the one-in-fifteen-million odds were for everyone else. I felt that my karma had to kick in sometime, that all the pain in my life must somehow be avenged if the universe was to make sense for me. So I thought I had a good chance. I did not. My chance was one in fifteen million. I lost, of course. Some toothless lady in Holopaw, Florida, won.

Gambling casinos feed on our incredible power to believe in our individual uniqueness and the just rewards waiting for us if we can only find them. And they fleece us over and over again like the sheep that we are. And because they compete with religions to capitalize on our willingness to believe in nonsense, most religions frown on gambling of any kind—that, and it cuts into their income.

Another way to see why nonsense has such a powerful allure is with the "cone of silence" analogy. The American television show *Get Smart* was a comedy about spies. One of the funniest bits was when, during a highly secretive meeting, the characters would activate the cones of silence. Clear plastic cylinders would descend from the ceiling and envelop each person within a completely soundproof environment. Then they would shout at each other and yell, "What?" until they became frustrated and deactivated the cones of silence.

Because the universe is far too complicated for any single human to attain a fundamental understanding of it, let alone an understanding of human history, we each live within a cone of ignorance. The reality we hold for ourselves is unique to each of

27

our bodies and how we have been raised (culturally indoctrinated). The only way to have a true communication with another person is to either base the communication on the most basic animal instincts, like sex or combat, or to communicate in a mutually understood system of rules (like math or baseball scores). Everything else, from how we feel about government corruption to what we think about the beauty of a sunset, is unique to us. There will always be people that can empathize and even agree with some of our views, but no two people share all views. We each possess a fundamentally unique and inaccurate perspective of the universe.

Another way to understand the necessity of using nonsense to grope for truth is with Plato's allegory of the cave in which people are prisoners, chained and unable to turn their heads. All they can see is the wall of the cave. Behind them burns a fire. Between the fire and the prisoners there is a parapet, along which puppeteers can walk. The puppeteers, who are behind the prisoners, manipulate puppets that cast shadows on the wall of the cave. The prisoners are unable to see these puppets, the real objects that pass behind them. What the prisoners see and hear are shadows and echoes cast by objects they do not see.

Plato lived four hundred years before Jesus. We have understood for twenty-four hundred years that our understanding of the universe and ourselves is pathetic, yet we love and fight, live and die passionately in the pursuit of our beliefs.

How can we believe in all this shadowy nonsense?

That's an easy one. There is no alternative. If you don't believe in anything, you won't get out of bed—you will just roll over and die. And, since we are far too puny to grasp even the basics of reality, we must create one for ourselves.

Douglas Adams masterfully described our puniness:

> The Total Perspective Vortex derives its picture of the whole Universe on the principle of extrapolated matter

28

analyses. To explain—since every piece of matter in the Universe is in some way affected by every other piece of matter in the Universe, it is in theory possible to extrapolate the whole of creation—every sun, every planet, their orbits, their composition and their economic and social history from say, one small piece of fairy cake.

The man who invented the Total Perspective Vortex did so basically in order to annoy his wife.

Trin Tragula—for that was his name—was a dreamer, a thinker, a speculative philosopher or, as his wife would have it, an idiot.

And she would nag him incessantly about the utterly inordinate amount of time he spent staring out into space, or mulling over the mechanics of safety pins, or doing spectrographic analyses of pieces of fairy cake.

And so he built the Total Perspective Vortex—just to show her.

And into one end he plugged the whole of reality as extrapolated from a piece of fairy cake, and into the other end he plugged his wife: so that when he turned it on she saw in one instant the whole infinity of creation and herself in relation to it.

To Trin Tragula's horror, the shock completely annihilated her brain; but to his satisfaction he realized that he had proved conclusively that if life is going to exist in a Universe of this size, then the one thing it cannot afford to have is a sense of proportion.

Our puniness requires us each to build and live in our own cloud of placating nonsense. We do this instinctively for self-defense.

Most religions have little tolerance for nonsense, except the brand they are selling. Most religions are intolerant of other religions, gambling, belief in the supernatural, or other nonsensical beliefs that can take the spotlight off their true nonsense. This intolerance will lead to their doom if we continue to evolve as a species. That is why some religions are against the idea of evolution, physical or cultural. These religions are on a long, slow path to extinction.

If you cannot embrace the idea of letting your mind and your reason lead the way for your senses and your nature, you are nothing but a sheep. If another person understands that you have the sheep quality, his or her nature will naturally want to lead you in the direction of his or her own benefit. You put yourself and the quality of your life in danger if you live by your nature—by your senses. You must discipline yourself to allow your reason to guide you.

6 DO I HAVE A SOUL?

Yes.

Most religions have a notion of the soul as some ghostly consciousness that inhabits your body like a renter. That is remarkably accurate.

Your soul is the sizzling, swirling, swimming electrons in your brain. That activity is your consciousness and your subconsciousness. It is what you think and feel. It is how and why you do what you do. It is the engine that processes everything you sense and the clerk that files your impressions and conclusions into a fuzzy, porous, high-capacity file cabinet.

When you sleep, that electricity is free to roam without the constriction of your direction, and the vacationing discharges form dreams. Even when your brain is taking a relaxing stretch, it is feeding you reality, albeit a dreamy one.

And when you die and your body is gone, most of your soul is gone. What remains are the impressions you have made on the world and the people you left behind.

In the Harry Potter books, the lead villain ensured his immortality by creating horcruxes, places that he could hide and protect the torn-apart pieces of his soul. By being a good parent, a good friend, a generous mentor, or an effective teacher, you do the same thing. The best part of you lives on in the people you affect. And the changes you caused in them become the part of their soul that are covered with your soul prints. That sentiment is now a greeting card, quoting Thomas Campbell: "To live in hearts of those we leave behind is not to die."

Your immortal legacy springs from the help and succor you give to others in their efforts to evolve themselves into their destiny. The ripples caused by your support and the waves made by your loving help become part of the living human fabric. This part of you that remains after your death will last longer than your tombstone. The more you reach out and support the evolution in others' lives, the longer and more sustainable your immortality will be.

Your soul is a bioelectric soup made over years of learning and feeling. It is the filter through which you experience God. The basic ingredients of the soup came from your mother and father, but the soup's quality is greatly impacted by the ingredients added during your lifetime. The amount and quality of the added ingredients is primarily governed by the amount of responsibility you take as the chef.

You have probably heard the term "old soul." It refers to a person who is wise beyond his or her years, has strong emotional stability, and seems to understand and be at peace with the world. I have met children with old souls, so I assume that a good part of a quality soul comes from genetics. But I have also seen people turn their bad lives into good, and their good lives into bad, so I know genetics are not everything. The one common characteristic that turns bad lives into good lives is responsibility. When individuals embrace their responsibility to craft their own souls, they evolve quickly. When they renounce their responsibility, their soup begins to spoil even quicker. And every person I have ever met with an old soul has had an incredibly powerful sense of responsibility. And not just responsibility for his or her own actions; he or she has also felt responsible for the shortcomings of others. This shows a deep connection with himself or herself and with others, and an expectation that we are supposed to strive for better. The old souls believe, with all their being, that we are destined for something better, and that it is our job to take the few steps we have time to take with wisdom, strength, and honor, and then pass the journey on to the next generation.

The most valuable souls take the hardest paths; those paved with responsibilities and problems.

Notice that I used the word *problems* and not the word *challenges*. *Challenge* is a new-age word that attempts to make a problem less threatening. If you are afraid of the word *problem*, I do not want you on my team solving one.

The quality of your soul is directly related to how hard you have worked to make it better. If you have made a long-term effort to increase your wisdom, to make wise promises and keep them, and to face and fight your demons, I will bet you are pretty happy with your soul. If you have not done these things, I will bet you are not as happy as you feel you should be and that you blame someone other than yourself for your unhappiness; you hold someone else responsible.

Your soul evolves during your life, mostly in jumps and starts. The biggest jumps are those that happen when you make your biggest decisions that go against your instinct—you do something that you could not have predicted. Something in your life experience mixes with your reason and you make a life-changing, gut-wrenching decision that scares the hell out of you. These are what I call "God Moments." These are the fleeting seconds that change the course of your life because you willed it so. I call these God Moments because they are the moments that decide and forge your future and God's. They are the rare instances where the random is randomized; the object that is already spinning on its pitch and roll is spun on yet another axis. These are the magic points in time when you take a giant leap forward—into the faith of yourself. At these times your wisdom, strength, and honor stand up from their repose, take a long, limbering stretch, roll up their sleeves, and stand ready for the problems you are sure to bring.

I remember sitting on my mom and dad's back porch after dinner one evening. I was thirty-four and had grown weary of traveling the country as a software mercenary. I saw an opportunity to create software that would serve a need in a small niche market. I knew it meant a year or two without income and chewing up my life savings, so I sought my dad's counsel. Dad had managed to escape a two-mule farm in the low country of South Carolina to become one of the primary players in an internationally respected organization. I always valued his opinions—they were typically thoughtful, farsighted, and reasoned. After talking it through, he told me that if my goal was to make money, and if I kept at what I was doing and invested wisely, I would retire a wealthy man. I remember telling him, "That's not the point. That's not what I want, not entirely. I want to build something!" He looked at me, wide-eyed, like a deer caught in headlights, and said, "Then you've made your decision. I'll help however I can."

That decision scared the hell out of me. But I felt like it was my road, and any other would be a betrayal to myself—and to God. I started the venture, and over the next few years I learned to take a beating. You name it, I took it. But I always knew it was the right path for me, so I did not mind taking it. In fact, the more I got beaten down, the more progress I felt like I was making. One day, about four years later, more money was coming in than going out. And a few years after that, I went to sleep one night and realized that I had built something that would be hard to wipe away. I think back and realize that when I blurted out that I wanted to build something, I wasn't really talking about a large software system or a business. I was talking about my soul.

You can increase the quality of your soul at any time. All you have to do is take on the responsibility and then do the work. Increase your wisdom. Clean your honor. Smite your demons, one at a time. Embrace your God Moments. And then show someone you love how to do the same. Villains shouldn't be the only ones able to make horcruxes.

7 WHY DO PAIN, EVIL, AND DEATH EXIST—CAN'T WE ALL JUST GET ALONG?

Pain, evil, and death apply evolutionary pressure—we aren't supposed to get along until the evolutionary process nears its end.

Saint Irenaeus, a second-century Christian bishop, said that evil is important and useful because knowledge of pain prompts humans to seek to help others in pain, and we would never learn the art of goodness in a paradise free of evil. In Hinduism, ignorance is the cause of evil and suffering from natural causes is explained as karmic results of previous births. Religions throughout time have done the same as governments—sought out simple things and complicated them.

I remember first asking myself the "pain" question when I was eleven. I was not much of an athlete, yet I still wanted to be good at baseball. No matter what I did, I was pitiful—I defined the word *suck*. As an eleven-year-old boy, I was very slow to grasp my own colossal lack of talent. In my myopic eleven-year-old mind, the reason why I struck out was because the pitcher threw to the inside, where I was weakest. The reality was that the entire strike zone exactly defined my weakest hitting area. And the reason why I missed a ball was because it took a bad hop. The reality was that all the hops that didn't end up in my glove were bad hops. The reality of my baseball skills fell well below my expectations. When reality falls below your expectations, unhappiness follows. I remember thinking, "Why does it hurt so much to be so crappy at something?" This led me to the next logical question, since I was raised a Christian and was taught to believe in God: "Why would a loving God let me be so crappy at baseball?" And then finally, "What is the point of pain?" I was empathetic enough to realize that my pain was not unique—I knew and had by then observed many examples of the pain of others.

I asked my mother why there was so much pain in the world. I don't remember her exact words, but the answer was something like, "God works in mysterious ways." I found this completely unsatisfactory, because, even at eleven, I knew that I was turning out to be someone that was not too keen on the spiritual God or mysteries. I stopped attending church when I was twelve.

The answer came in my teens when I learned physical ailments, from paralysis to nerve and brain damage, could completely block a person's sense of physical pain. People so afflicted are taught to be very careful and hyperaware of their surroundings because they can be mortally wounded and not even know it. The loss of your sense of pain is a loss of a primary guardian of your well-being. Pain hurts in order to get your attention so that you can alter your behavior to save yourself. Pain is your friend. Pain is good. Pain exists solely for your well-being.

The amount of pain floating around in the universe is exactly the amount needed to keep the fingers of two-year-olds out of flames and to keep the rest of us from poking ourselves with pointy sticks. There is a lot of pain, but it is not too much—it is just the right amount to alert us that something is wrong and could become FUBAR.

In the next answer I will define evil as anything that goes against your way. Evil is just another form of pain, and pain can be good for you. Death can be good, too.

Death ends life and provides it with a limited duration. Almost all known forms of life have a life span. Some exceptions are *Turritopsis nutricula* (the potentially immortal jellyfish) and the giant redwood tree. Both have the ability to live ridiculously long lives, but the rest of us have worrisomely short life spans. Why do almost all living things have built-in life spans?

Simple. To give new lives a chance to make the species better more quickly.

Evolution depends on the cycle of life and death to move a species forward. To quote from Charles Darwin's *Origin of Species*:

> *Effects of Use and Disuse.—From the fact alluded to in the first chapter, I think there can be little doubt that use in our domestic animals strengthens and enlarges certain parts and disuse diminishes them; and that such modifications are inherited.*

Darwin gave example after example of how a new physical feature in an individual was God's way of randomly trying out an idea. If the random new feature, or mutation, allowed the animal to fit better into its environment and breed more effectively than its peers, that mutation would have a good chance of being passed on. But it takes the death of the old generation and the birth of the new generation, round and round, like a diesel engine that just keeps going, to accomplish evolution. If humans lived to be five hundred years old, human evolution would slow to a crawl.

Death is good because it quickens evolution's rpm (revolutions per millennium).

Apparently, *Turritopsis nutricula* and the giant redwood tree are near the end of their evolution, so the pressure of a short life span has been relaxed.

This is a good place to say a word about the pain death causes those left behind. The sense of loss can be incapacitating. And if the death was traumatic, dramatically untimely, or morbidly unjust, it can shake your sense of karma and fairness to the core. But as painful as it is, those feelings bring out two blessings. First, you are likely to re-acknowledge how tenuous your grasp on life is and to focus on, at least for a little while, how incredibly lucky you are to be alive. Second, people are being born every day, bringing new hope to our potential for achieving our destiny. The human tide goes in and it goes out, and with every cycle we make a little progress.

Pain, death, selfishness, and bigotry all exert pressure needed to cause us to think, decide, and evolve. H. G. Wells's protagonist in *The Time Machine* said, "*It is a law of nature we overlook, that intellectual versatility is the compensation for change, danger, and trouble. An animal perfectly in harmony with its environment is a perfect mechanism. Nature never appeals to intelligence until habit and instinct are useless. There is no intelligence where there is no change and no need of change. Only those animals partake of intelligence that have to meet a huge variety of needs and dangers.*"

It is probably obvious to you that our species is nowhere close to the end of its evolution. We have a lot farther to go. Our bread is far from done. If you want our species to reach its evolutionary zenith and be the best bread it can be, do not whine about the heat in the oven.

8   WHAT ARE GOOD AND EVIL?

Good and evil are points on the compass in the pilothouse of your way.

Evil balances good in the human weather system.

Our life is a set of perceptions and the way in which those perceptions are processed. The driving force behind a life, or "the meaning of life," is the need for a life's way to be shared by as many other lives as possible, whether the sharing is done through procreation and genetics, tyranny, or surrender and adoption of another's way. This explains why an amoeba undergoes mitosis, why trees make seeds and warn other trees of danger, why dogs have puppies, why people have children, why male lions kill the young of a newly acquired pride, and why a man seizes power of a country and kills millions of its population under his rule.

Why can't we all just get along? Everyone promotes his or her way, and promotion through tyranny evokes the automatic and inalienable right to defend one's way. The word *tyranny* evokes an image of a mighty ruler who cuts off heads and puts them on pikes. But a tyrant can be as puny as a child that cuts in line at the cafeteria. Tyranny and the defense against it are the driving forces behind human events. Just like the heat of the sun and the pull of the moon are the driving forces behind the weather, the tension and compression between tyranny and the defenders of liberty shape human drama and create the human weather system of competing high-pressure and low-pressure ways.

Each life promotes its way. The basic actions involved in promoting a way are through defense, trade, or offense.

Liberty is the right to enjoy your way as long as it does not preclude another life from enjoying its way. It is natural to defend a way against attacks. It is natural to defend your liberty. If someone tries to dictate any part of your way (your appearance, your belief or value system, your relationships, your goals and dreams), it is only natural that you should resist.

If you are not actively defending your way, you may be looking to improve it through studying and trading with the ways of others. In this fashion, you may voluntarily trade components of your way for the hope of a more satisfying or happier way (like converting your religion, or admitting to being gay, or giving up your carpentry business and earning an engineering degree).

According to Athos, Alexandre Dumas's philosophical musketeer, "*People, in general, only ask advice not to follow it; or if they do follow it, it is for the sake of having someone to blame for having given it.*" I would like to add that people, in general, give advice not so much as an aid to another, but because it promotes their own way.

If you are not engaged in defending your way, or in trading parts of it, you are probably inflicting your way on others (rooting for a football team, bombing abortion clinics, or spanking your three-year-old child).

Good is everything that goes your way. Evil is everything that

41

goes against your way. A person breaks into your house in the middle of the night and attempts to kidnap your daughter. You kill the intruder. You have acted heroically for your family, risking your life to preserve the life of your daughter. You have done good work. Society won't punish you (at least most won't). However, the intruder's family has no reason to believe the events occurred as you described and will pursue you as a murderer. They will continue this pursuit until they are convinced you acted in a good way.

Good and evil exist only in the way north and south exist. They are directions that only matter given an orientation. North and south don't mean anything in outer space. Good and evil only make sense when the way that they polarize is clearly understood. From a personal point of view, good is for you and evil is against. But the idea of good and evil can be used more generally in regard to the forces that act on liberty.

Hitler was a hero to millions (and is still a hero to some), a standard-bearer who promised a new world position to Germany of the 1930s. He was so highly thought of by the German people, who were emerging from the disastrous results of the Treaty of Versailles, that some thought he was an angel. This man ultimately caused tens of millions of deaths and was seen by most of the rest of the world as the most evil man alive. The struggle for fascism /communism against democracy in the last one hundred years is a great example of the struggle between ways, and how the directions of good and evil change based on the way you are going. The concepts of good and evil are widely used to label the forces attempting to protect or destroy liberty.

The struggle between the takers and defenders of liberty provides the pressure required by the crucible of human cultural evolution. We will never be ready for our destiny as star trekkers if our cultures don't progress, and culture only progresses after enough of its individuals entice it into the future.

We don't get along because our cultures are still cooking. We are nowhere near done. Our conflicts, battles, wars, struggles, transgressions, and misdemeanors are just symptoms of our need to domineer and our nearly fathomless ignorance. We need to keep the pressure on because no one yet has found *the way*.

The ideas of heaven and hell are closely related to the ideas of good and evil. But heaven is not a place that exists, like some kind of five-star spiritual resort where your every whim is indulged, nor is hell a place where you go to spend eternity suffering through your worst nightmares. Heaven is the place you make for yourself and your loved ones—it is the moments of peace and sublime happiness that occur in your life from time to time. When strung together they make a very personal heaven, made sweeter by how hard you worked for it. Hell is the regret, the shame, and the self-loathing you live with after making shortsighted, easy, unwise, and dishonest decisions. So it is true, metaphorically speaking, that your soul does go to heaven and hell, but in truth it visits both places and is far more mobile than scripture leads us to believe. And when you are dead, your soul goes to neither place, but remains in the horcruxes (see answer to "Do I have a soul?") that you have created during your lifetime.

Your soul is a ship on a vast and tumultuous ocean, filled with other ships like yours. Some are going your way, but most are not. Those that are going other ways are likely to get in your way. They will be evil to you, and you will be evil to them. If you parley and compare notes with open hearts and wise heads, you may learn a better course from each other. But this is unlikely, because following your own compass just feels so good. So we will crash into each other, year after year, until enough ships, a critical mass, make it to the destination we all really wanted—they find *the way*. When those souls get to that shore, they will need to build a lighthouse and patiently wait as the last of the lost ships sink, crash into each other, or find their way home.

When we have reached our evolutionary zenith, we will have peace. Before that, God will keep peace out of our hands. God made us to find it, and we will not look with enough enthusiasm if

43

we are comfortable.

God knows that comfortable people rarely do great things. That's why so many of us are so very uncomfortable.

9 WHY ARE PEOPLE SO SELFISH AND BIGOTED?

If a person's way is to survive in the high-pressure crucible of the world, it must be protected and advanced by fierce advocacy.

Life is selfish. People are selfish. Everyone is selfish. That is how it has been and how it is. I sound cranky, don't I? After I explain myself, I won't seem cranky, and you will understand people and yourself much better. You may be even able to love everyone.

Take, for instance, Mother Teresa, known for her unselfish work in Calcutta. To quote her, "I heard the call to give up all and follow Christ into the slums to serve him among the poorest of the poor." This would seem to be complete proof that I am wrong—not all people are selfish. But wait. According to *Webster's*, the word *selfish* means "seeking or concentrating on one's own advantage, pleasure, or well-being without regard for others." I think it would be fair to Mother Teresa if I said she pursued her famous work because it satisfied her. Her self-worth was based on how she did the work. She was rebellious in how she tactically approached the work, going against many of the church's rules. It was of great personal value to her to do her work her way. It pleased her to do this, just like it pleases a trophy wife to brag to her girlfriends about her new jewelry. Mother Teresa did her work concentrating on her own advantage, pleasure, and well-being, without regard to others in the church. Her work happened to be helping the poor, whom she held in high regard, because it pleased her to do so. Others that she felt hindered her work or disagreed with her approach, she held in low regard. I am not saying that Mother Teresa was evil or more selfish than average. She simply did what she wanted to do and became famous for being a selfless person.

Hitler, on the other hand, is widely known as selfish. If the art world critics of Vienna had shown a little more love to him in the 1920s, the 1940s would have been a lot quieter. I am sure that, from Hitler's point of view, he sacrificed for his beloved country that had been raped by Europe and the United States with the Treaty of Versailles. Clearly, such sacrifice would be deemed unselfish. The small detail that millions had to die for Germany to achieve greatness was probably rationalized in his mind as so many things are within the mind of a truly ambitious person. I don't think Hitler was any more selfish than Mother Teresa, but because he systematically moved local decision making to a central and powerful location, he was exponentially more evil because he was so big a force, not counter to an unjust force. Hitler was a world-class, liberty-squashing thug.

Normally, the difference between someone deemed as selfish and someone who is not is just a matter of short term versus long term. If you watch a child repeatedly giving up his or her share of candy to a sibling, you would deem the child unselfish. But if you found that after doing that many times, the parent treated the unselfish child to a special treat to acknowledge the behavior, it might be safe to assume that the child was being unselfish in the short term to selfishly benefit in the long term.

Some of the most ruthless, tyrannical people I have ever met pride themselves on throwing charity functions. They do this for the prestige, of course. If they really wanted to help the charity without drawing attention to themselves, they could. But they don't. They don't give to help the cause, even if that may be a by-product. They are just customers at a store that sells prestige. They are unlike Abraham Lincoln, who in 1832 wrote, *"Every man is said to have his peculiar ambition. I have no other so great as that of being truly esteemed of my fellow men, by rendering myself worthy of their esteem. How far I shall succeed in gratifying this ambition is yet to be developed."* And in the winter of 1841, in the midst of his deepest depression, after his most intimate friend Joshua Speed warned him that if he did not rally he would surely die, Lincoln replied that he was more than willing to die, but that he had yet *"done nothing to make any human being remember that he had lived, and that to connect his name with the events transpiring in his day and generation and so impress himself upon them as to link his name with something that would redound to the interest of his fellow man was what he desired to live for."*

Prestige is what you feel when you drive your Mercedes by a homeless person. Esteem is what you have if you find the homeless person viable, useful work and get him on his feet again. We are all out for ourselves, either in the long term or the short term. Even the fellow that jumps on a grenade to save his buddies is really trying to save a world where heroes are revered—he hopes his buddies will help build that world. Being able to judge the quality of someone's selfishness will allow you to stock your life with friends and loved ones who will enrich your life and to keep out the lowly prestige seekers that will pollute it.

Do not waste your time wishing for someone to be punished for his wrongdoing. If a person has demonstrated over time a character of weakness, dishonesty, and ignorance; has left a trail of destruction in the wake of his or her life; has hurt you repeatedly without making amends; then it is time for you to extricate him or her from your life. Punishment will find this person on its own without your assistance. In my experience, such people are unhappy and don't know why—they live in hell and die there. You don't need to pile on—just get out of the blast zone.

As Charles Dickens wrote in *Oliver Twist*, "*If when we oppress and grind our fellow-creatures, we bestowed but one thought on the dark evidences of human error, which, like dense and heavy clouds, are rising, slowly it is true, but not less surely, to Heaven, to pour their after-vengeance on our heads; if we heard but one instant, in imagination, the deep testimony of dead men's voices, which no power can stifle, and no pride shut out; where would be the injury and injustice, the suffering, misery, cruelty, and wrong, that each day's life brings with it!*"

If Mr. Dickens was still around, I would tell him that injury and injustice, suffering, misery, cruelty, and wrong, are all still right here, doing fine. Ruthless people don't contemplate and consider the harm they cause; they are naturally dumb to it. God gave them that protection to belay their natural fears and give them what on the surface appears to be the courage to do their deeds. But it is not courage—it is their natural blindness to the consequences of their actions. Ruthless, shortsighted people are like hand grenades going off; anything in the area will suffer sharp devaluation—it is what they were made for.

You must understand that selfishness is natural, just like bigotry is natural, and then try to understand the role they play in your life and the lives around you. Only then can you fashion effective shields from them.

Bigotry is a driving force in cultural evolution. It is instilled in our nature so that we will promote our adopted way. If we are too weak-minded or weakhearted to define our own unique way, and most of us are, we fight for the way we have adopted. This is a good system for evolution because strong ways provide strong indoctrination and weak ways do not. If a new way comes along, it must be intuitively valuable so that it will be immediately appetizing—it must sell easily. And even then, the creator of the way must be very strong to promote it in the face of the current, popular, powerful ways.

Bigotry is deeply ingrained in our nature for two reasons: our natural inclination to categorize and our natural need to feel superior. If all other things are equal, you will prefer your child to another, your football team to another, your political party to another, your state to another, your country to another, your whatever to another. Bigotry is the key component that traps each of us into our own cone of ignorance. Bigotry is a natural force, and, as with gravity, to fly you must learn to overcome it for short periods. It is on these short flights that your most important epiphanies will occur.

If you understand why selfishness and bigotry exist, you will not be so quick to loathe those in whom you see these qualities.

Loathing crowds out love.

Understand. Tolerate.

Loathe less.

Love more.

10 WHAT IS HONOR?

Honor is your hook on which others hang their trust.

Most children are taught honor by being punished when they lie.
But few are taught what honor is, when it is valuable, and when it
is not. Honor has come to primarily mean public esteem. The word
comes from the Roman god Honos, the god of chivalry, honor,
and military justice. It has also become a word to mean integrity or

a keen sense of ethical conduct. Honor is of primary value in creating and preserving societies because there can be no trust between individuals without individual honor. The cement that binds free people together is trust. An individual's honor is the hook on which others hang their trust.

But if honor is so important, why is it valued less and less? That's a simple question to answer, as long you understand that there are three basic types of human relationships, and honor is only important in one of them. Peer-peer relationships are the type most of us are familiar with, where both individuals freely enter into and choose, on an ongoing basis, whether or not to stay in the relationship. Honor and trust are keys to the good health of these relationships. However, there are two other types of relationships where honor has little or no value: master-slave and foe-foe relationships.

In the master-slave relationship, constant and overwhelming force is required of the master and yielding is required of the slave—honesty is not a factor. In the foe-foe relationship, each side tries to do the most damage to the other until one side is defeated—no honor is required. If you have relationships with people that are devoid of honor, don't kid yourself; they are not peer-peer relationships or friendships, but either master-slave or foe-foe. To be fair to yourself, you should stay in a relationship only if you know what it really is and are satisfied with it. The reason honor seems to be valued less and less is that more and more of our relationships are becoming either master-slave or foe-foe, where honor is a burden, not an aid.

In Niccolò Machiavelli's words from nearly five hundred years ago: *"Everyone understands how praiseworthy it is in a Prince to keep faith, and to live uprightly and not craftily. Nevertheless, we see from what has taken place in our own days that Princes who have set little store by their word, but have known how to overreach men by their cunning, have accomplished great things, and in the end got the better of those who trusted to honest dealing."* Machiavelli clearly understood that powerful people must put on a show that they value honor so that their slaves, who believe themselves to be peers, will not feel like slaves. But to keep that power, they must rely on cunning, not honor. Powerful people realize how important honor is to their subjects, but are very careful never to indulge in honor themselves.

As the world becomes more sophisticated and our cultures make real progress, it will take higher and higher degrees of cunning to fool the people. Master-slave relationships will be revealed more quickly and more easily, and the slaves will naturally work to break the chains. But master-slave and foe-foe relationships will exist as long as we remain fundamentally human. Honor will have a limited yet important place in our future, as peer-peer relationships hopefully predominate the others.

We will never achieve a state of being where honor is pervasive until there is no more conflict. To be honest with an enemy is to hand him easy victory. Even if we evolved to a cultural utopia where conflict among ourselves was rare, we would still need to maintain our ability to fight an enemy and to lie. Without our ability to guard ourselves, if we ever meet a rival species, they will destroy us.

11 WHAT IS TRUTH?
Truth is comprehensive, accurate knowledge.

Buddhism has the Four Noble Truths:

1) Life means suffering.
2) The origin of suffering is attachment.
3) The cessation of suffering is attainable.
4) The path to the cessation of suffering exists through gradual self-improvement.

If you are not a Buddhist, you will notice that some noble truths are missing. For instance,

1) Sex feels good.
2) Everyone dies.
3) Football is more fun to watch than baseball.

So you can see immediately that the idea of truth is nothing more than that: an idea.

How would any of us know how to gauge the accuracy of information that did not have our own self as it source? In my life, I have seen many stories published about which I had personal knowledge, and in *every* case, the published story had, in the best case, small lies, and, in the worst case, great big whoppers.

Even in your personal experiences, you must admit that your memory of them is filtered by your soul and your extremely limited senses. If you watch a football game, you cannot keep your eyes on every player at all times—there is too much going on for you to get a detailed and comprehensive sense of the game. You normally follow the ball during the play. If you were asked what each player's role in the play was, you would be ignorant.

Each of us only takes in a small sliver of what is going on. And we understand and process a fraction of that. We should be truly grateful that, as we each stumble through our foggy existence, we don't do more harm than we do.

Truth is currently unreachable—that's why we reach for it so hard.

The common idea of truth has therefore evolved to mean not philosophical truth, but rather the opposite of a lie. Go to *Webster's*, look up *truth*, and you will not see the word *accuracy*, but instead the words *sincerity* or *fidelity*. The establishment has successfully rebranded the story that truth is a matter of loyalty. So let's explore this brand of truth.

In this code snippet, truth is required for the software to work:

```
If HeartBeating()
Then TakeBreath()
Else BeStillandRot()
```

The functions in the above software snippet return true or false. In software, true exists as a one. Its nemesis exists as a zero. This is the closest thing to truth that I have ever experienced, because the truth we allude to in daily conversation is tricky.

The truth we talk about on a daily basis does not exist, other than as an expression of how small a lie is or, in other words, how loyal you are to what you really believe.

A thermometer measures heat because there is no such thing as cold—cold is just a human way to measure the pain caused by the lack of heat. In this way, we should not think about truth as a thing, but rather as an esoteric way of sizing and weighing a lie or how far you maliciously deviate from what you believe.

A proud math student tells you that two times three equals five. He is not a liar. He is an idiot. Give him a loaded Glock 17 with the high-capacity mag and there will be blood. But give him a village missing its own idiot and you will have peace.

In order to tell a lie, all that must be done is to pass on information that is **believed** to be false. If you tell someone that two plus two equals four because you don't want him to know the real is answer is five, you have told a lie. When the world went into Iraq because Western intelligence agencies believed that Saddam Hussein possessed weapons of mass destruction, many people believed that George W. Bush lied to the American people about the existence of the weapons. But if George believed the reports about the weapons existing, then he did not lie, because he believed the intelligence himself. If he did not believe the intelligence, then he did lie. We will never know which one it was.

Telling the truth is impossible—but telling your perception of the truth is expected of an honest person. A person who knows that his or her truth is just a shadow of the real truth is a wise person. And a person who tells no lies is rare, if not a myth.

The vast majority of humanity lives with the soothing delusion that they understand—that they might not know everything, but they know the majority of the important things. A tiny minority grasp the magnitude of their ignorance; that billions of people came before us of whom we know little; that there are millions of books in thousands of libraries that we have never read; that many of the problems we face today were faced in the past and solved. But we don't care, because if those people were so smart, why did they die? We are comfortable with ignorance because it is our chronic condition—we have made peace with it.

We are a mean, cunning species that knows truth is out there. But more importantly, we know that judicious management of knowledge leads to individual riches.

Knowledge, truth, lies, public relations, spin, perspective, bias, bigotry, and our own powerful yet hidden urge to see our way win all mix together to make clear sight of reality very difficult. Cunning people take advantage of this to fashion and sell everything from soap to war. That is why the idea of truth has lost much of its luster, and why gifted liars live so well—at least for a time.

12 WHAT IS LIBERTY?

Liberty is the amount of freedom you enjoy while living within a group of people.

If you find yourself alone on a beautiful island, you have complete freedom. There is no need for a measurement of freedom because you have all that there is. You can sing at the top of your lungs, run around naked, mark all the trees with urine, poop in the middle of a clearing, and eat with your mouth open. You are also free to be eaten by a wild creature, succumb to a jungle bacteria easily cured by medicine you don't know how to make or take, and die of exposure, starvation, scurvy, tetanus, dehydration, boredom, or loneliness.

When you live with people, you exchange some of your freedoms for privileges. Your curbed "civilized" behavior buys you a level of security from your community. As you give up more freedom, you enjoy more security from the community. You may even become entirely dependent on the community for the necessities of life—

you may become a pet or even a slave.

The great political struggle in my day is centered on liberty—the ever more sophisticated and powerful state is taking ever more freedom from the individual, worldwide, in what is extensively publicized as progress. And worldwide, individuals are rising up and pushing back. In the Middle East it is called "the Arab Spring." In America, both sides—those in favor of more central government and those for less—are realizing that their elected officials are out for themselves. And all over the world the outcome will be the same as it always has been when the people finally throw off the yoke of tyranny. Once the people's passion ebbs, new tyrants will always be there to step in using the new rhetoric of the day. It's happened in France, China, Russia, Cuba, Venezuela, North Korea, Sudan, Zimbabwe, etc. It will continue to happen until the political class is subjected to annual reviews and subsequent rewards or punishment. And since the political class makes the rules, this day will not come until the vast majority of individuals are more independent and liberty-minded.

In order to understand human events, it is useful to create an abstract model of the main objects and forces that manipulate them. As in weather modeling, we can define the main object being acted upon, such as air, and the main forces that act upon it, such as heat from the sun. Of course, the modeling process is far more complex than this, and it really relies on the oodles of accurate measurements and oodles and oodles of mathematics and computer cycles. But in the end, the models that predict the temperature and rain percentage for tomorrow are just abstract representations of the true atmosphere. It is high time we used our affinity to understand our universe and point it toward human social interaction in an attempt to demystify it.

First, we must find the central object in human events that is being acted upon. What thing more than all others is sought after, protected, stolen, battled for, and causes deceit, murder, alliances, hate, and love?

Is it money?

Human conflict was around long before money was invented. (Besides, money is just a socially accepted way to store labor.)

Is it prestige?

Most people will not risk their death, the death of their families, and the death of their nation over an issue of prestige (when defined as a high social standing). Why would people over the millennia risk not only their own lives, but also the lives of their families and the fate of their nations? It is more than prestige.

Is it power?

We would have to admit that some societies, like that of the Vikings, would risk everything for more power (when defined as the ability to control other people). But we are looking for the one thing that all people throughout time have treasured more than anything.

Is it survival?

That must definitely be a part of it, but people have gone to war and risked survival to protect the things that were important to them. Aha! Maybe that is the key. If what people go to war for is to "protect the things that are important to them," what are those things? They must be valuable enough for someone else to want to take them. There is a word for these things.

Liberty—the condition of being free from restriction or control; the right and power to act, believe, or express oneself in a manner of one's own choosing; the condition of being physically and legally free from confinement, servitude, or forced labor.

Most people will agree that each of us has the right to air. So far, this has not been widely bottled and sold. Throughout human history, air has been free for the taking, so let's assume that this is a liberty that humankind accords to each of us. Thomas Jefferson would call this right "inalienable." Now, let's suppose that a big burly beast—we'll call him Mongo—chokes off your air supply by a steady application of his foot to your throat. You will of course resist the efforts of Mongo to keep you from your air supply. What are you willing to do? Think about this for a minute. Wouldn't you be frightened, maybe panicked? All those years of free air intake have come to an end and your lungs begin to burn. Mongo's foot has stolen your undeniable right of breathing. That foot has got to go. As the fear subsides, a feeling of rage begins to overtake your panic. You begin to wrestle with the foot. Something deep inside you knows that you need the air, and, more than that, you have a right to it. The panic is nearly gone. A feeling of righteousness now supports your rage. You are fighting against evil, fighting on the side of good. You are supposed to win. You take out your fountain pen and thrust the sharp end deeply into Mongo's ankle. Mongo has now had one of his liberties stolen (the right to choose what you want pierced). Mongo quickly calculates how many more liberties he will need to sacrifice in order to continue to steal this one liberty from you. He retreats, comforting himself in the thought that there are other people's air supplies that can be choked off without such bristling defense systems as yours.

The establishment of liberty and its subsequent defense from an attacker is the core of the human weather system. With a thorough understanding of liberty, human events may be understood more completely.

Liberty is a fairly new concept to human consciousness. When the founding fathers of the United States of America hammered out the Constitution in 1787, many of them saw a real danger that their species (to be more precise, Americans) was too young for liberty; that the common person was not evolved enough to participate in his own government. The majority of academics and the political class still think that way—that is why teachers are not evenly distributed among the political parties.

During the end of the 1700s, the Western world had an epiphany—that our species was ready to take the next step in our cultural evolution. The philosophers of the Reformation led the way in a fresh look at our reality, and what followed over the next two hundred years was more cultural evolution than had occurred in the previous ten thousand years. The very existence of the idea of liberty was the source of this incredible push forward.

Why was the idea of liberty so late in coming? Let's look at history in a simple context that focuses on the evolution of liberty.

Humans began as little more than apes struggling to walk upright. The idea of liberty was as far off as algebra. If you wanted something, you took it. If you wanted to keep something, you protected and defended it. It appears we began as social beings, so it follows that we could rely on others for defense, food gathering, and procreation, but the underlying thought in human consciousness was that life was fleeting—you had to fight or be prepared to fight for your existence at all times. The fight you lost was the event that wiped you from the canvas of existence, as you would wipe a small stain off a painting.

At some point in human events, another way to take and secure liberty became apparent—politics. It was possible to convince a naive person to release his liberty. You did not need to take liberty—you could make the holder decide to give it up of his own free will by promising him something he thought was more valuable, like food or security. One branch of politics, business, was to become the next big thing.

Let's say you and your friend are walking through the jungle looking for food. It is thousands of years before Christ, and looking for food in the jungle is something you do a lot. All of a sudden, your friend happens upon a banana and picks it up. It is now his banana. He is at liberty to do what he pleases with his banana. How do you get that banana? If you had no grasp of politics and you thought you could get away with it, you would take the banana. You would bash your friend's head in and eat the prize right over his still and faintly breathing body. But when your friend woke up, your quality of life would plummet. If you had used your political skill, you would have worked to convince your friend to give you the banana by trading something for it. A little quid pro quo can mitigate retaliation—you probably want your brains in your head rather than all over the rock in your friend's hand.

The most honorable and enjoyable political coercion is the bargain, where both sides agree on a deal, something for something, quid pro quo, then execute the deal. Both sides in most cases are satisfied at the end of such an episode. Another type of political coercion is the promissory deal. That is a deal where one side gives up his liberty now on the promise that the other side will do something later. If the promise is not kept, or a disagreement results concerning what the promise actually was, the person who gave up his liberty is left with nothing, not even the dignity of a bashed-in head.

Darwin's theories of evolution are widely accepted and, when applied to early human cultures, can logically show what would and did happen. Tribes that evolved cultures that increased their ability to acquire food, establish security, and reproduce are the cultures that outlasted the others. Although the cultures that evolved are more varied than shampoo brands, all cultures were based on power—acquiring and preserving it. And the number-one way of acquiring power was by taking it. Battles and wars are what people did instead of commerce. It was the main course of human events from the time these began through the beginning of the 1800s. And then, just as when Jesus turned the philosophical side of human consciousness from hard bargaining and revenge to generosity and tolerance, the Western human consciousness began to question if war and conflict were the best ways to promote a culture. The use of politics to acquire and secure power was still very popular, but one form of politics, business, was beginning to show unexpected qualities. Through trading goods and services, people began to rely on other people for necessities. Our very livelihoods no longer rested upon our ability to dominate people and take the products of their toil. Our livelihoods now rested on our ability to provide goods and services needed by the people who *bought* our goods and services. And the most remarkable thing of all happened. A very large part of the human consciousness realized that the average person is unlikely to kill a good client.

As the predominant human relation becomes that of the bargain, and something is *always* given for something, we will slooooowly say good-bye to our days of bashing one another over the head for gain. But the head-bashing days are still with us, and the tool of choice for robbery is no longer a club, but government, and the bashing is not done with a big stick, but with laws and taxes.

13 WHAT ARE MY NATURAL RIGHTS?
You have the right to try to survive.

Consider a squirrel, sitting on a tree branch, munching on a nut. What are its natural rights? Does it have the right to an education? No. Does it have the right to health care? No. Does it have the right to food and shelter? No. Does it have the right to clean air and water? No. And the peregrine falcon just above it knows that the squirrel does not even have the right to life.

Your natural rights are the ones God gave you, which are exactly the same as he gave to the squirrel.

Religion, like government, has been making simple things complicated for a long time. In *The Rights of Man*, Thomas Paine discusses two types of rights: natural and civil. He opines that every civil right grows out of a natural right. But Mr. Paine begins with the incorrect assumption that natural rights are *"the intellectual rights, or the rights of the mind, and also all those rights of acting as an individual for his own comfort and happiness, which are not injurious to the natural rights of others."* I can assure you that if you are the only human living in a jungle, when a tiger pounces on you while you sleep and begins to crush your windpipe so that its breakfast will stop fidgeting, Mr. Paine's natural rights will not occur to the tiger. That is because they exist only in the minds of other humans—just like Santa Claus and unicorns.

But wait—you have been hearing all your life about "your rights." Well, you do have some rights. They are called **civil** rights, and they are nothing more than the collection of personal liberties you enjoy as long as you play your role in **civil**ization. Your civil rights are yours in exchange for being a member of civilization and playing by its rules. These rights are your payment for keeping your part of the bargain.

The United States clearly and simply states the rights it promises to its citizens in its Constitution, where both the president and Congress can easily find and ignore them.

The United Nations has a list of human rights. They give us thirty of them. Article 25, Section 1 is particularly generous: *"Everyone has the right to a standard of living adequate for the health and well-being of himself and of his family, including food, clothing, housing and medical care and necessary social services, and the right to security in the event of unemployment, sickness, disability, widowhood, old age or other lack of livelihood in circumstances beyond his control."* In order to provide these goodies, the wealth required must be *taken* from someone. Eventually that someone is going to be upset and realize that some of these so-called rights are really just claims on the labor of others. There comes a time when that lazy son-in-law has finally used up the last shred of your hospitality and you need to do what's best for him and you—throw him out. When someone realizes he is enslaved, he tends to push back on the master's right of ownership.

I like to think of rights in two ways: the right to control oneself and the right to control others.

The right to control oneself causes conflict only when it spills over into affecting another.

The right to control others exists only through bargaining, coercion, or force, and lasts only as long as those being controlled continue to enjoy the arrangement or are too weak to throw off the yoke of control. The right to control others is the eye of the largest storm in the human weather system.

However, the right to control others is essential to creating large works. Cities, highways, automobiles, electronics, movies, and any large work that takes many people to create are possible only with the right of one to control others. So, at once it is the right that allows us to build things much larger than ourselves, and the right that could most easily destroy us.

Harriet Beecher Stowe wrote about the enslaved poor in *Uncle Tom's Cabin*. Ayn Rand wrote about the enslaved wealthy in *Atlas Shrugged*. When people feel that others hold invalid rights over them, they will fight back. They will either strike at their masters or they will run.

Your civil rights are yours only as long as you continue to hold up your end of the bargain, and only as long as you are able to defend yourself from trespasses upon them. Guard them dearly, because when they are gone, what remains are your natural rights, which are the same rights God gave to squirrels and bacteria—the right to try to survive.

14 IS CENTRAL POWER BETTER THAN DISTRIBUTED POWER?
No. Both should exist in balance.

After years of traveling the country as a consultant on large software projects, I stumbled onto an opportunity to build and sell my own software. The code grew to millions of lines and was guided by local decisions of bright and concerned users coordinated by myself.

Each instance of my software and database resides at the client's location and is automatically updated by a central server at our office in Florida. We can read and update the data and schema of every distributed database and can update each software instance one at a time, in groups, or everywhere. This architecture allows us to take and satisfy requests for new features and deploy them to our clients the same day, and in some cases the same hour. The features are distributed in four ways:

Locally selectable—each client can choose to turn the feature on and off.

Locally on—the feature is always on for that client until he asks for it to be turned off.

Universally selectable—the feature is made a core part of the software and is available for everyone to turn on and off.

Universal—the feature is made a part of the core software; it's on for every user all the time.

For over fifteen years, we have delivered as many as fifty new features a week, to hundreds of sites across the country, serving thousands of end users. And clients have been able to tune their systems to their unique requirements without negatively affecting other clients. On occasion, a request for a feature to the core software is such a good idea that all other clients enjoy the innovation.

And during those fifteen years, a clear pattern has emerged. The clients that routinely reevaluate their processes and request new features enjoy thriving businesses, while those that simply rely on the innovations produced through the requests of others tend to go out of business. It has become apparent that clients that make local decisions to solve local problems are also the best ones at helping to solve the problems that affect the entire client base.

I settled on the distributed architecture after spending years in large corporate information technology departments where people spent the majority of their time serving their careers rather than their user base. I can recall countless instances of users not being at liberty to do their jobs because a critical function on their computer had been disabled by an overly cautious IT department.

In the early years, when we trained and installed our software on-site, I ran into a phenomenon I named the Breezeway Effect. The headquarters office (HQ) for one of my clients, where billing and payroll for nine offices were conducted, happened to be very close to one of the "front" offices, which provided direct client service. The only thing that separated the two offices was a twelve-foot breezeway where people could smoke. During the installation of our software, I worked very closely with both the HQ office and the front office and found the personnel in both locations to be hardworking and bright. However, the two locations had very different perspectives. The HQ staff thought the staff across the breezeway was a collection of pirates and monkeys, and the front office staff looked upon the HQ office as a courtly promenade of humorless dullards. Both staffs discounted the other's worth because they were ignorant of the value the other staff provided. And neither staff was interested in curing its ignorance.

It's necessary that I understand the processes of both offices in order to install my software and provide training, so I understood they could not survive without each other. The HQ had simply become the home of all processes that were "factored" out of each office. One location to process the payroll with its nearly endless rules is far more efficient than nine locations doing the same. The HQ location can grow more expert and more efficient, and the company saves money. However, the nine locations served very different client pools and worked with various types of employees, so these processes were naturally left distributed. The business naturally grew that way because the owner was constantly tweaking operations to save money. And from what I saw, the nine locations loosely coordinated by the one HQ office worked efficiently. There was a constant organic flow of process responsibility from distributed to central and vice versa. If a new industry requirement materialized and caused a new process in all nine locations, that job would normally become an HQ job. But if the requirement affected just one or two sites, normally those were the only sites that would ever hear about the new process.

When too much money and decision making move to a central location, a warning sign of the imbalance will be complaints from the citizenry regarding the difficulty in conducting their business and their lives. This was an actual comment on an article in the *Wall Street Journal* regarding the growing difficulty of running a business in the United States:

> *How many people does it take to change a lightbulb in fundamentally changed America?*
>
> *One is needed to research which lightbulb company is the most environmentally friendly, has employed the most minorities, and has contributed to the political campaigns of the correct party.*
>
> *Two union members are needed to hold the ladder so that OSHA standards are met and so that the individual union members don't get lonely.*
>
> *One lawyer is needed to draft the liability release that the owner of the old lightbulb must sign relieving everyone associated with the lightbulb-changing project of any liability or responsibility for damages, nonperformance, or lack of passion.*
>
> *One Ivy League academic is needed to study the effects of altitude and social pressure on the person that will climb the ladder to change the lightbulb.*
>
> *One social worker is needed to offer counseling to the lightbulb changer once he descends the ladder with the old lightbulb and attempts to reenter society.*
>
> *One person is needed to create a disposal plan for the old*

lightbulb that includes a public relations campaign that highlights either the brief or epic life span of the lightbulb, whichever one is in the best interest of the project manager.

One lobbyist is needed to pressure Congress to pass laws making it illegal for lightbulbs to burn out and to tax all people who don't have any burned-out lightbulbs to support those suffering from burned-out lightbulbs.

One person is needed to testify before Congress regarding how many jobs will be created by the burned-out lightbulb, and another person is needed to lobby for a new government program to call for early burning out of lightbulbs as a national stimulus to the economy.

One person is needed to write a book called Burned-Out Lightbulbs and Justice, a systematic and peer-reviewed proof of how people suffering from burned-out lightbulbs can be made to feel better and more valued and thus the whole culture lifted into a new era of justice if only the people with unburned-out lightbulbs would burn out their lightbulbs more quickly.

Three people are needed to demonstrate against the project because the place where the old lightbulb died is obviously historically important and should be restored and kept empty to commemorate the life of that lightbulb and others that it represents. In a pinch, this can be cut to just two people, but it can be scientifically proven that a demonstration with three members is up to 50 percent more effective than one with just two members. Proof of this can be provided with a small grant of $50,000.

One person is needed to study how many jobs were created or saved in the course of changing the lightbulb.

So that is 1 + 2 + 1 + 1 + 1 + 1 + 1 + 2 + 1 + 3 + 1, or 4.5 million. If this mission of hope and change is successfully *funded, we will eventually need to add one more person because we need someone to actually change the lightbulb.*

These figures are just estimates—we are waiting on actual figures from the Congressional Budget Office, but we are confident that if a lightbulb is burned out and the audacious and courageous decision is made to in fact replace the lightbulb as an investment in our future, enough jobs can be created to pay off the national debt as long as the project continues through the next presidential election.

This post shows that even when people are frustrated with burdensome central government, they can still keep their sense of humor.

Friedrich Hayek wrote nearly half a century ago about the "pretense of knowledge." Central decision makers assume they have enough knowledge to make the best decisions. They do not. Their arrogance is dwarfed only by the complexity of our world.

Centralized control leads to fiscal problems because of the human vermin attracted to large piles of money. If you place ten billion dollars in a pile and wait, you will see it attracts the most ruthless, cunning, corrupt, nefarious swath of humanity imaginable. The kind of people naturally attracted to the possibility of easy money are exactly the sort of people that inhabit Washington, D.C., and other capital towns. If the money piles are kept smaller and more local, you no longer must deal with the world-class scoundrels, but merely the local variety. If your community is unlucky enough to have a world-class scoundrel, then at least only your community has to suffer. But since all the suffering will be felt by your community, it will be much more likely to dispatch said scoundrel.

Centralized money breeds corruption. If you want more corruption, centralize even more. If you want less corruption, take the power and the responsibility for that power back to your state or town and watch it like a hawk.

If we are to achieve our destiny of millions of humans traveling through space on thousands of ships, we have *loads* of progress to make. It is my direct experience that the optimum amount of human progress is made from the leaps afforded by individual innovations. Localized decision making leads to faster and higher-quality innovation. The assembly line, the idea of God, the computer, the automobile, flight, and rocketry are all stories of individual genius building on the work of prior genius. Centralized decision making is best left for gargantuan, otherwise duplicated, and mundane work projects.

15 IS LOVE MORE POWERFUL THAN HATE?

Yes, over the long haul.

Many great quotes have been fashioned about the power of love, but they tend to be esoteric and lack the quantitativeness I was after when I asked this question all those years ago. So this is a two-part answer.

Regarding the first part, love is the emotion that tightly binds us to the ones we love. Love prejudices us against those that don't share our love or, worse, disagree with our love. College-football fans have been known to shoot each other in parking lots over disagreements about their arbitrary love. In those parking lots, love was the wellspring of the hate that pulled the trigger. And the hate most definitely won, in the short term. But one dead football fan does not diminish the power of the football team—it may actually work to promote the brand of the slain and tarnish the brand of the slayer.

Hitler used hatred to bind and focus the German people. It worked well for nearly a decade. But hatred is an emotion that burns brightly and consumes its host—only short-term works can be fueled with it alone. Although Hitler's main theme was hatred and retribution, he wove in love of the homeland and of the people, and kept a steady stream of information and imagery flowing. The two-pronged attack enchanted the German populace, and few escaped with their lives or their honor.

Jesus is widely credited as the single most successful promoter of the power of love. In the Bible, Matthew 5:44, Jesus said, *"But I say unto you, Love your enemies, bless them that curse you, do good to them that hate you, and pray for them which despitefully use you, and persecute you."* It takes a boatload of love to treat an enemy well. But the payoff is that someday you may turn the enemy into an ally, or even a friend. The downside may be that your enemy sees this kindness as weakness and accepts the invitation to further persecute or even destroy you.

To summarize the first part, a long life steered by love will be more valuable than the same life steered by hate. I know that is not the answer that was sought. So let me get to the real answer in part two.

Force makes humans and humanity move—literally. Some force is loving, or just, and some is hateful, or unjust. Which is which is the rub.

Power is a word an engineer knows to mean work done over a period of time. And work is an amount of force exerted through a distance. So, "Which is more powerful, love or hate?" can be answered best in engineering terms. And it comes down to the most effective type of force: a loving force or a hating force.

The force used to bring a hungry baby's mouth to a nipple would be widely regarded as a just force. Any force opposing this just force would be considered an unjust force. Now, consider the difference between forcing a hungry baby's mouth to a nipple and forcing a hungry, lactose-intolerant adult mouth to a bottle of milk. Both forces are no longer just, are they? The two are different because one is felt to provide a liberty (a baby's want of milk) and one denies it (a lactose-intolerant adult's right to avoid milk).

Force exerted in the protection of liberty is just, while force that attacks liberty is unjust.

So the power of love and hate comes down to your perspective of liberty. Do you think that you should be allowed to do *anything*, as long as it does not directly affect another's liberty? If so, you are a libertarian. Or do you think that things you do that *might indirectly* affect another should be unjust? Let's say you are raped and you want to end the pregnancy that ensues. You will be directly affecting the liberty of the baby, but it is completely dependent on you for its life, so the liberty of the baby is debatable. However, other people will be appalled that you took the life of your baby and will feel that the moral standard of their society is degraded— they are indirectly affected by your decision to abort the baby.

Things get murky very quickly if we attempt to enjoin actions that *indirectly* affect others.

The only just force is that which counters unjust force.

Unjust force is at work everywhere and is widely accepted as just: forcing private businesses to have handicapped parking, drafting people into the army, requiring people to belong to unions in order to work, bombing abortion clinics, forcing people to change the meaning of the word *marriage*, making people use fluorescent lightbulbs, enjoining people from using drugs in the privacy and safety of their home, prohibiting people from arming themselves for protection, and on and on.

We have not evolved as a species enough to see the injustices clearly. One day, when the majority can clearly see and think, and are strong enough and wise enough not to be so easily steered, the libertarian ideals will take hold. But not yet—we are too early in our evolution. For now we can only light beacons—we can, in Bob Marley's words, "light up the darkness." If enough of us live in love and liberty, others will be drawn to the light.

In 1800, the population of the United States was just over five million. A little over two hundred years later, the population is more than 310 million and still growing. This amazing growth has one cause: the promise of more liberty.

Many years from now, just forces will outshine unjust, generation after generation; the lopsidedness of the results will burrow deep into our minds and cultures. There, somewhere in our wonderful future, the majority will wake up to the evolutionary beacon of liberty. Then, and only then, will we be ready to go where we are destined to go.

Liberty will win.

Love will win.

16 WHY DO OTHERS HAVE SO MUCH MORE THAN I?
Because God wants us to race to it.

We are herd animals, deeply aware of the pecking order. We feel good when we are better than another and bad when we are worse than another. This feeling varies in strength among individuals, just like the abilities to crack a differential equation or sing beautifully. The people that are naturally driven by pecking order placement who also have other gifts—like intelligence, tenacity, cunning, and creativity—will most certainly achieve feats and accumulate wealth with far more success than the average person.

Life exists to progress in reaction to the stress in its environment and to morph into something that fits better. Most of the stress on a member of a society comes from the other members of the society. We are in a natural competition, a race, made more complicated by rules laid down by the successful competitors that came before us. If you are successful, you will be able to remove some of the outdated, arbitrary rules and replace them with some of your new arbitrary rules.

The race is strict but not malicious. Its point is to extract the best ideas from the entire stock of humanity and implement the ones that have the most force behind them.

Some people, unsatisfied with their performance in the race, will naturally try to change the nature of the race. This is natural and just, because the race must evolve like everything else. People satisfied with their performance in the race will resist changing the rules of the race. And some people will see an opportunity to work as warriors for one side or the other. In political terms, and generally speaking, conservatives preserve the race and liberals change it. A healthy, balanced struggle between the two helps the race evolve so that it constantly adapts to better serve its purpose, and that is to apply pressure to both the individuals and the social structures of the human species so that we all evolve.

It is one of the toughest things in life to see other people born better than you. One thing you can count on is that there will always be someone that is prettier, faster, smarter, richer, funnier, stronger, or more popular than you. But here is the single biggest reason that this should not bother you: the person that you envy envies someone else. And we are all competing with one another for the evolution of our species—something that helps us all.

It is a real miracle you are here—I proved that in the answer to "How Did It All Begin?" Everyone else is here to goad you into finding your purpose. Enviable people surround you on purpose. God put them there to get you off your soft backside and cause you to find your destiny.

One quick word of warning: there are people who specialize in brokering excuses to the masses of people that have deficits of strength, wisdom, and honor. These people will tell you that your lack of happiness and worldly possessions is not your fault, but rather the fault of a crooked system—a rigged race. If you hand these people the reins to your life, your search for your purpose will come to an end. Don't let that happen. You are a miracle and completely unique. You were created with a destiny, but it is up to you to find it—and you won't find your true self on that sofa.

Don't waste your miracle—do not hand someone else the reins to your life. Your destiny evaporates the moment someone else gains control of your rudder.

Everything is the way it is. God has set itself on a path to self-discovery, and we are a very important part of that—maybe the most important part. If God must piss you off with envy to get you moving, is it really a bad thing? Beside, once you have worked, risked, and innovated enough, you will be the focus of the envy of others—and maybe because of their envy of you, they will get off their flat, static posteriors and move forward.

17 IS LIFE WORTH IT—IS THE PLEASURE WORTH THE PAIN?
Yes!

Even with the demons that have haunted my life, I can honestly say that the pleasure has far outweighed the pain.

In my youth it was my oversensitivity that allowed in what I thought was too much pain. The pain was caused by my constant shock at the difference between reality and my expectations. To become an adult, your soul must be hardened, just like steel, so that you can face and survive the challenges of a valuable life. At nineteen, I remember how tired I had grown of the hardening process. I did not know I was close to the end of the worst of it. I had no way of knowing. And I couldn't go through much more. I made a promise that saved my life and allowed me to begin a long and wonderful adventure.

I am not saying that I would want to go back and relive a single day of my life. No thanks. I like it right here, right now, thank you very much.

But there came a point where my expectations became more pragmatic—they fit reality well enough that the constant shock from my expectations rubbing on reality was replaced by a sporadic but palpable tingle. What would have caused great pain to the younger me, I now found to be an interesting annoyance. So, in my pleasure-pain ledger, the pace at which the pain column gained entries slowed. And the entries that did make it there were less severe. And the pace at which the pleasure column gained entries quickened.

This quickening process of the soul has been acknowledged and written about for hundreds of years. In Daniel Defoe's *Robinson Crusoe*, the protagonist's relationship with God had grown from nearly nothing to something real and useful, when he contemplated his blessings on the second anniversary of his island solitude:

> *It was now that I began sensibly to feel how much more happy this life I now led was, with all its miserable circumstances, than the wicked, cursed, abominable life I led all the past part of my days. And now I changed both my sorrows and my joys: my very desires altered, my affections changed their gust, and my delights were perfectly new from what they were at my first coming, or indeed for the two past years.*

Falling in love with my wife; the birth of our two children; the time and laughter we have shared; the beautiful place we live; the wonderful people I work with and for; the incredible future I see for my family and my country and my species; the pleasure column now towers over the pain column. It is no contest anymore—it's a slaughter.

If you are a new adult and your pain column currently has the upper hand, take comfort in the fact that you are on the right track. The tide will soon turn. I was in my late twenties when it turned for me. But everyone is different. You must simply have the courage and the faith that your tide will turn. And the more pain you have truly felt and allowed to harden your soul, the more able you will be to face the big problems that will certainly find you if you aspire to a valuable life. Let your soul mature into a filter that protects you from the small pains and magnifies the little joys. The pain column will languish and joy column will swell.

Hang in there. The light will come. The day will dawn that you will look back at your life with awe and pride, and a deep appreciation and gratitude that the younger version of yourself had the strength to soldier on.

In the immortal words of Dory, the regal tang fish in the movie *Finding Nemo*, "Just keep swimming, just keep swimming."

18 CAN I BE HAPPY?
Yes, but you should learn two tricks.

I learned these tricks through years of trial and error, and most things I tried failed spectacularly. The first trick is very effective and quite easy. The second trick is even more effective, but a lot more difficult.

First, always have something to look forward to. It can be as elaborate as a trip to a foreign land or as simple as a walk in the park or a hug from someone you love. It really doesn't matter, as long as you will honestly look forward to it. I think this works for me in the same way the saying "One hand for you, one hand for the ship" works for a sailor. Looking forward to something is your one hand for the ship. Somewhere deep in your mind it supplies security, in that it gives value to the time that passes leading up to the anticipated event.

During the first few years of starting my business, I spent spans of weeks afraid that I would waste my time, my effort, and my family's future on my gamble. I spent countless hours in airports and hotels realizing I would never get the time away from my family back, and yet I knew my gamble would pay off because I was completely unwilling to fail.

During the darkest times, I would tell myself, "Everyone has to be somewhere doing something, and here you are doing what must be done to accomplish what you want. Suck it up." It became a mantra and it worked. Looking back, one of the reasons it worked is that I knew I was inching toward a life where I would spend more time with my family and have more control over my life than if I were an employee. I was looking forward to my dream of my business being successful enough that the daily fear would subside to a manageable level. And the freedom provided by owning my own business is everything I thought it would be and more. I still can't believe I made it through the doubts and the fear and the dark hours when it appeared all was lost. But I did. And the person I was back then somehow knew I would make it. That person latched onto this future and forged it into reality. I can't thank that person enough. That person made me very happy.

Second, you must learn to manage your expectations. Happiness is the difference between what you expect and what happens. If you set your expectations too low, what happens will not be as great as what could have happened. And if your expectations are set too high, what happens will certainly be disappointing, if not crushing. It takes a lot of practice to set and continually reset your expectations to maximize your accomplishments yet minimize your disappointment.

Ennui is a word invented by the rich to complain about their boredom right in front of the help. Most of life is boring because it is spent in transition scenes that join the juicy bits together. If your life were a movie, 99 percent would be edited out—and I am being kind.

However, do not discount the value of these transition times, because these are exactly the times when knowledge about yourself and the world (God) morphs and reboots. My philosophy came to me in pieces over many years during these times—while shaving, brushing my teeth, washing my hair, walking, waiting for a woman to get ready, mowing the lawn, driving, sitting in an airport, changing a lightbulb, or waiting for my bowels to move. The transition scenes in my life made me who I am—those millions of moments fashioned my soul.

If you are dreadfully bored during your transition scenes, I advise you to always have a question in the back of your mind. If your brain has nothing better to do, it will naturally set itself onto your question. If you make a habit of this, you will soon discover that epiphanies find you with regularity.

That's my advice on how to be happy, but there are times to set happiness aside. Some things in your life are so important to your soul that you must do them. Sacrificing your dreams so that your children can have theirs is not as common as it once was, but it still happens. Soldiers are still jumping on grenades to save their buddies. Accepting true diminishment in your life so that someone you love can survive will not bring you a normal happiness, even if you live through the experience. But it does earn you the immortality that comes from leaving an indelible imprint on the soul of the person you helped. As I said in the answer to "Do I Have a Soul?" villains shouldn't be the only ones able to make horcruxes. When a horcrux is made by a person with much wisdom, strength, and honor, it becomes a beacon to the living, a guide to the good path, and a source of immortal comfort.

19 DO I MATTER?

Yes, but how much depends on your choices.

In 1999, John Rawls was awarded the National Humanities Medal by US President Bill Clinton. Mr. Rawls authored *Justice as Fairness* and other political-philosophical works, and his work is the center tent post of the redistributive and affirmative-action movements in the United States. Using Rawls's "veil of ignorance" concept, the progressive new-age morality justifies commandeering money from its earners and moving some of it to the disadvantaged (a good portion stays with the people who did the commandeering).

What is this mystical philosophy? Specters sitting behind a "veil of ignorance" negotiate the social laws they will live under once they take possession of their bodies. Because they are ignorant of the bodies they will assume, they do not know if they will be born rich or poor, pretty or ugly, adroit or ungainly, pink or brown, weak or strong. This ignorance forces them to deal fairly in setting up the social structure, so that no matter which body they get, they will have an equal chance at having a life with good and fair access to the necessities and good and fair access to opportunities to improve their station. Mr. Rawls wrote extensively about how "justice as fairness" and the "difference principle" could and should be applied to social policy for the greater good of all.

There is a disagreement in how to apply Rawls's theories. For instance, behind the veil, two societies are considered, each consisting of three people. In one society each person has ten dollars. In the other society, two people have eight dollars and the other has twenty dollars.

Group one will choose the society where everyone has ten dollars.

Group two will ask why the one person in the second society has twenty dollars and what opportunities exist for the others to earn more money. If satisfactory opportunities exist, group two will take the second society.

Group one focuses on fair outcomes because they are immediate, tangible, and easily presented to the masses. Group two focuses on fair processes because outcomes are fleeting but processes can go on and on, evolving and progressing as they go.

The purpose of life is to advance the universe into its next form. The purpose of an individual life is to move itself, its family, and its community forward to the next form. Life is about movement and is the most powerful randomizing agent in the universe. We must concentrate on making opportunities available to every individual so that we can maximize the mobility of each person. Each individual is a living process producing daily, weekly, monthly, and yearly outcomes of pain and pleasure, success and failure.

Focusing on outcomes impedes mobility, progress, and evolution. It feels better to force an outcome because it feels good to exert power and have a quick result—the gratification is immediate. But the only just force is one that counters an unjust force.

Taking wealth from one group and giving it to another is a very tricky business—search Monty Python's Dennis Moore on the Internet for a hilarious illustration.

It takes respect for the universe and a patient understanding of time-dependent processes to understand that a good process will continually yield fair outcomes.

We must focus on fair processes. We know when processes are fair because there will be more fair outcomes. It will take constant tuning to keep the processes fair, so that outcomes continue to be fair. It is as wrong to focus purely on fair outcomes as it is to take the A grades from a good student and give them to a bad one.

Redistribution of labor's rewards retards evolution and suspends progress. People that promote redistribution are antiprogressive. It is the ultimate irony that the current Progressive movement in the United States promotes antiprogressive policies.

Are the economic and social processes in the United States currently fair? Well, more fairness is certainly possible. There are now only a few dozen ways out of the poverty cycle. There should be millions. Libertarians should be leading the effort in creating new pathways out of poverty. Small businesses need to create more internship and apprentice positions to get our young people firmly positioned on the first rung of the economic ladders. Money must be attached to each student so that a student's family can fire a school , enroll their child in a better school, and the money for that student will follow. Broken schools will either get fixed or be closed and great schools will expand. And to get a high school diploma, each young person should demonstrate a basic understanding of how the government of the United States works—the same way a naturalized citizen demonstrates his knowledge. This should be viewed as a basic self-defense class, because without it, our new adults are like lambs to the slaughter.

Ignorance and sloth in the citizenry lead to corrupt leadership. Ironically, we are all born as ignorant sloths.

We have suffered too much corruption under politicians, regardless of the label they wear. It is time to focus on redistribution of opportunities rather than redistribution of outcomes. And we cannot rely on our political representatives to do this—it is not in their best interest, because their political power comes from buying votes from one group of voters with the money taken from another group of voters.

Creating fairer processes in our culture is up to each of us—individually. Only when we demand more fairness in our trades, professions, media, families, and communities will our culture truly start to progress. The most harmful philosophy to human progress is the idea that outcomes should be manipulated to produce temporary, fleeting, and, in the end, counter-progressive social fairness. John Rawls would not be pleased with the way his teachings have been used.

So what does this have to do with the question "Do I matter?"

We are at the dawn of a new war between the individual and the state. It is being waged globally. If the state side wins, evolution will be set back many, many generations. That setback may be enough to end us.

God needs each individual to matter if we are to have a good chance at finding it. Centrally controlled decisions are less organic, less dynamic, and ultimately less likely to be genius, or even innovative. And it is going to take a string of genius innovations, over a long period of time, to find God.

On your deathbed, I can assure you that you will not look back and congratulate yourself for all the risks you averted, and all the battles you ducked. Your self-esteem at your end of days will come from the risks you took and the battles you fought for the ones you loved.

God needs you.

You must matter.

20 WILL HUMANITY MAKE IT?
Nine to five, yes.

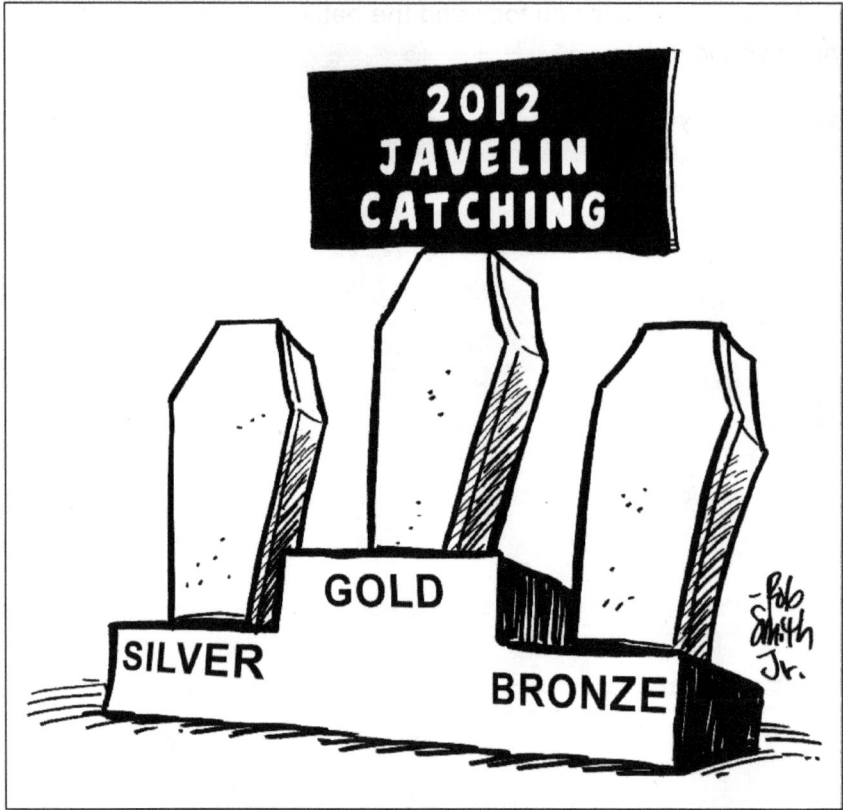

In about twenty generations, or about five hundred years from now, we have the potential for a stunning future. Hundreds of ships, each holding thousands of scientists, engineers, and trades people, will be making their way through our galaxy, turning over every interesting cosmic rock they meet, in a powerful push to understand God. These fleets of ships will have enough people to be viable, self-sustaining, ever-evolving human colonies. Some people may never visit Earth in their lifetime. At this point, the future of the human race will be almost assured because of its distributed instead of centralized nature. For the first time in human history, it will take more than one large meteor to annihilate the human race.

And when I say "ships," I am not talking about those you have seen before. I am talking about vehicles that mimic the planet—on the scale of the Gerard K. O'Neill design.

The technology it will take to achieve this stage in our evolution is much greater than has been displayed in the *Star Trek* and *Star Wars* movies. We will have the ability to move billions of tons of material off the earth and other planets at a small fraction of its current cost. We will need to do this in order to build the massive fleet of ships that it will take to safeguard our species and whisk us through the stars. So, in order to achieve this future we will need to do something incredible: we must figure out a key ingredient of God. We must fundamentally understand force and, to be more specific, gravity.

Science currently recognizes four types of force: gravitational, magnetic, and the strong and weak nuclear forces. In order to go star trekking, we will need something that we currently do not have—a thorough knowledge of gravity. We have laws, like

Newton's, that help us predict the effects of these forces, and yet we do not know how to mitigate and manage them. For instance, the force of gravity causes a mass of any size to accelerate toward earth at the rate of 32.2 feet per second every second (or 9.8 meters per second every second). We can calculate the force that masses exert on each other as a function of their mass and their distance from each other. But for nearly a century, we have been trying to create antigravity, with little success. The Institute for Gravity Research of the Göde Scientific Foundation has tried to find reproducible experiments that demonstrate an antigravity effect. The foundation has offered a reward of one million euros for a reproducible antigravity experiment. Apparently, that reward is not juicy enough, because it has had no takers.

We will have a breakthrough in gravity research sometime in the next ten generations (about 250 years from now). We do not belong in space before we have earned a rigorous knowledge of gravity. Doing so would be like setting out into the Atlantic Ocean armed with nothing more than arm floats and a childlike sense of wonder. The only real benefit our space industry has achieved is satellites, and when you get down to it, all it takes to put one into orbit is to throw it hard enough in the correct direction. We could have done that with a large trebuchet and some small rockets.

We will achieve a breakthrough in gravity theory because two things will act as a pincer movement in the next ten generations. The first is global overpopulation, and the second is indescribably powerful computers.

About five hundred generations ago, it is estimated that the world's population was roughly one million. We are now seven billion souls. Our population has increased seven thousand times. Without serious constraining pressure, Earth's population will quadruple by 2100. We will be living on top of each other. As the population pressure builds, the motivation to seek out new human habitats will explode.

The computer I first spent significant time with (called a VAX) used

94

two megabytes of memory to host eighty users. My new phone has sixteen gigabytes. The power of computers has increased by eight thousand times in thirty years. Computers in one hundred years will be more than one hundred million times more powerful than what we have today. Software will take advantage of that new power. Computers and software will be the main tool used to unlock the secrets of gravity. Because of the pressure exerted by overpopulation in one hundred years, enough scientific, engineering, and computing resources will be devoted to gravity research, and we will begin to crack the nut.

I believe we can achieve this kind of monumental feat in the next 250 years because of what I have seen during my lifetime.

I have watched while the "baby boomer" generation of the United States attempt to sell their collective selfishness as "social justice," and I have watched the subsequent generation judge them for it. This latest attempt by a group of people to subjugate the labor and intellect of one group so that they can control another group has been tried again and again, all over the world, since we emerged from feudal times, and has always ended with the same results. The people whose labor and intellect was stolen rise up and end the theft. Eventually, the state is forced to understand how to work a checkbook and live within its means.

The oscillations between state and individual power started over ten thousand years ago in massive swings, and in the last one hundred years, the swings have been between communism and dictatorships. The wave height for these oscillations is reducing, indicating that we are zeroing in on the inevitable balance of power between the state and the individual.

And this makes sense, because the power and success of the state flows directly from the power and success of its individuals. The speed at which the state evolves is un-severable from the speed at which its individuals evolve. The most successful states are those that foster the most successful individuals, and, in their culture and dogma, celebrate the value of individual innovation and achievement over the massive power of concerted and cooperative state efforts. When the state garners too much power, cultural evolution grinds to a halt because the individual innovators are unmotivated. When the state surrenders too much power, large-scale, concerted efforts lack the cohesiveness needed to succeed. Either balance between the two is maintained, or human progress is thwarted.

Like a water molecule is to its drop of water, a single person is to his or her culture. The characteristics of a water drop follow the characteristics of the makeup of each molecule and how these molecules interact. If the integrity of one molecule unzips, a chain reaction can ensue, and it is the end of the drop of water.

For people, strength, wisdom, and honor do not come naturally. They are traits hard-won through years of fighting against the current of sloth, swimming against rivers of fear, and searching through the darkness of ignorance. Every small bit of hard-earned progress, day after day, year after year, is the sum total of a person's journey toward God. The sum total of a person's wisdom, strength, and honor is the distance he or she has covered from his or her natural, animal self toward his or her destined being.

The amount of strength, wisdom, and honor in each of us dictates the power of our culture and its ability to achieve the major social, technological, and economic breakthroughs required to attain our destined future.

A people get exactly the state they are able to build and maintain. No other state is possible for them for any length of time. The state reflects the strength, wisdom, and honor of its people. If you buy a bum mansion, it will become a hovel in a short time. The person that earns the mansion through time and effort will keep it up nicely.

Look into yourself. How strong are you? How wise are you? How honest are you? Answer each of these questions for yourself.

Now you provide an answer: will humanity make it?

AFTERWORD

The years I spent searching for and arriving at these answers
were transformative. As a child and a young man, I thought of
myself as "me." Bad things happened to me. Things frightened
me. The world was a rough place for me. I was overwhelmed and
felt like a victim, and, just like the word *me*, the object of a
preposition, I always felt like I was on the receiving end.

As I lived my life, somehow I found a little courage to take risks,
and I slowly discovered that the drive to achieve was within me
the whole time. As my wisdom gradually grew, my strength grew.
As my strength grew, I took more risks, and found that staying the
course through temptations and trepidations yielded great
rewards. I found that honor was not a platitude or a vague notion,
but a character trait that the cream of humanity is drawn to like a
flame. And honor led to riches.

And one morning—I don't remember when—I woke up thinking "I,"
not "me." I was going to do some great things. I was going to work
through my fear. I was going to rough up the world. I was going to
figure things out.

This transformation to thinking about myself as "I" instead of "me"
is the key that saved my life. I went from being the object of a
preposition to being the preposition itself. I understood in my soul
that the only limit to how much I could change the world was how
much strength, wisdom, and honor I was willing to bring to bear.
The practical outcome of everything I cared about was within my
control.

Because the "me" to "I" transformation brought about by my
answers, I call my philosophy "I-ism."

If you are at that time of your life where you are feeling
overwhelmed and think that the pleasure is not worth the pain,
please, for God's sake and yours, understand that you are smack

in the middle of your quickening process. Don't make rash decisions during this time. Your bread's not done. Let it bake. Think about the answers I have provided and then come up with answers of your own—better answers. You will find your purpose. You can have an extraordinary life—if you choose to. And, if you are worth your salt, when you are old, you will help a young person get through the same hell you conquered.

SELECTED BIBLIOGRAPHY

Adams, Douglas. *The Ultimate Hitchhiker's Guide*. New York: Wing Books, 1996.

Bullock, Alan. *Hitler: A Study in Tyranny*. New York: Harper & Row, 1962.

Cupitt, Don. *After God*. New York: Basic Books,1997.

Darwin, Charles. *On the Origin of Species*. CT: Easton Press, 1963.

Defoe, Daniel. *Robinson Crusoe*. Norwalk, CT: Easton Press, 1976.

Dickens, Charles. *Oliver Twist*. Norwalk, CT: Easton Press, 2004.

Dumas, Alexandre. *The Three Musketeers*. Norwalk, CT: Easton Press, 1978.

Durant, Will. *The Story of Civilization: Our Oriental Heritage*. Norwalk, CT: Easton Press with the permission of Simon and Schuster, 1992.

Farrington, Karen. *The History of Religion*. New York: Quadrillion Media LLC, 1998.

Goodwin, Doris Kearns. *Team of Rivals*. New York: Simon & Schuster, 2005.

Hawking, Stephen. The Illustrated *A Brief History of Time*. New York, NY: Bantam Dell Publishing Group, 1996.

Machiavelli, Niccolò. *The Prince*. Norwalk, CT: Easton Press, 1980.

Meriam, J. L. *Engineering Mechanics*. Vol. 1, *Statics*. New York: John Wiley & Sons, 1978.

O'Neill, Gerard K. *Human Colonies in Space: The High Frontier*. Princeton, NJ: Space Studies Institute Press, 1989.

Paine, Thomas. *Rights of Man*. Norwalk, CT: Easton Press, 1979.

Rand, Ayn. *Atlas Shrugged*. New York, NY: Random House, 1957.

Rawls, John. *Justice as Fairness: A Restatement*. Cambridge, MA: Belknap Press of Harvard University Press, 2001.

Rowling, J. K. *Harry Potter and the Half-Blood Prince*. New York: Scholastic, 2005.

Snow, C. P. *The Two Cultures*. Cambridge, UK: Cambridge University Press, 1959

Stowe, Harriet Beecher. *Uncle Tom's Cabin*. Norwalk, CT: Easton Press, 1979

Twiss, Miranda. *The Most Evil Men and Women in History*. Singapore: Michael O'Mara Books, 2002.

Van Doren, Charles. *A History of Knowledge: Past, Present, and Future*. New York: Ballantine Books, 1991.

Wells, H. G. *The Time Machine*. Norwalk, CT: Easton Press, 2002.

Odin and Ymir—http://www.gly.uga.edu/railsback/CS/CSOdin&Ymir.html.

Space Colony image—http://www.nss.org/settlement/space/stanfordtorus.htm.

www.ingramcontent.com/pod-product-compliance
Lightning Source LLC
Chambersburg PA
CBHW061754020426
42331CB00006B/1472